THE ULTIMATE SANDWICH BOOK

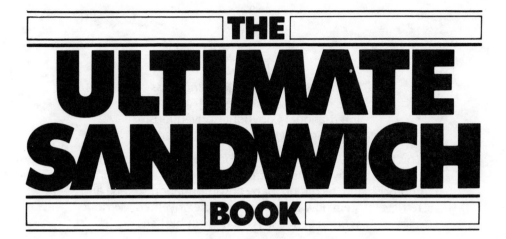

THE ULTIMATE SANDWICH BOOK

WITH OVER 700 DELICIOUS
SANDWICH CREATIONS

by Louis De Gouy, et al.

RUNNING PRESS
PHILADELPHIA, PENNSYLVANIA

International representatives: Worldwide Media Services, Inc.,
115 East Twenty-third Street, New York, New York 10010.

9   8   7   6   5
Digit on the right indicates the number of this printing.

LIBRARY OF CONGRESS CATALOGING-IN-PUBLICATION DATA

De Gouy, Louis Pullig, 1869-1947; et al.
The ultimate sandwich book.
Includes index.
1. Sandwiches   I. Title
TX818.D42   1982   641.8'4   82-537
                                            AACR2

ISBN 0-89471-164-4 (paperback)
ISBN 0-89471-163-6 (library binding)

Revised and edited by Elizabeth Zozom and Samuel Hughes
Cover design by Jim Wilson
Cover photography by Carl Waltzer
Typography by Comp-Art, Philadelphia, Pa.
Printed by Port City Press, Baltimore, Md.

This book may be ordered from the publisher.
Please add $1.50 postage.
But try your bookstore first!

Running Press Book Publishers
125 South Twenty-second Street
Philadelphia, Pennsylvania 19103

Table of Contents

Introduction

Though it's been around for a long, long time, there is something almost quintessentially American about the sandwich. It's casual, convenient, and incredibly adaptable, equally at home in the lunchbox, the all-night diner, and the hors d'oeuvres tray. The laziest bachelor and the most inspired epicure can both make a sandwich to their liking, and since its contents are limited only by the imagination, the sandwich seems pretty likely to survive any changes in the public mood.

Chances are we'd be enjoying sandwiches today even if the gambling table hadn't been invented, but they wouldn't be called sandwiches. After all, it was the gambling table that prompted the fourth Earl of Sandwich (1718-1792) to have his food served to him between two slices of bread so he wouldn't have to interrupt his gaming to eat. It was a wonderful idea, and since he was kind enough to bestow his name on it, it's tempting to give him credit for the whole thing and be glad he didn't put a patent on it.

Actually, though, people were munching on various foods stuffed between slabs of bread long before the earl came into the picture. Arabs had been filling the pockets of their delicious pita bread with various meats for centuries. The ritual of eating chopped herbs, nuts, and apples placed between two slices of matzo—symbolizing Egyptian mortar and the suffering of the Hebrews before their deliverance from Egypt—has been observed by Jews at Passover for over 2,000 years. And there were probably other, earlier versions as well.

It's been more than 40 years since Louis De Gouy published his **Sandwich Manual for Professionals,** and while there have been some changes in the way we eat, his recipes are just as tasty today as they were in 1939. De Gouy was something of a genius at the art of sandwich making, and his book—from which most of these recipes were taken—was intended for the professional who had to serve food that a wide range of people really like to eat. There is no more telling bottom line than this, and whether you're a professional, a novice, or an inspired amateur, you should have a lot of satisfied customers on your hands with these recipes.

We've added quite a few new recipes to this book, and the result, we feel, is a collection of the best sandwiches of the last 50 years. They range from contemporary creations involving pita bread and soyburgers, to older classics using fruits and jellied meats, to regional favorites like submarines and cheese steaks—even novelty **un**-sandwiches such as ice cream sandwiches and some delightful variations on the theme of French toast. In other words, the works. We think you'll have fun with this book, as well as a lot of happy eating, and after all, that's what sandwich making is all about.

PART 1

Elements of the Sandwich

Basic Ingredients

Sandwich making is usually a fairly casual enterprise, but it helps to be at least passingly familiar with the huge variety of ingredients available to you. Given a sandwich's basic building blocks—bread, cheese, fish, and meat—your opportunities for experimentation are literally infinite.

Bread, for instance, comes in a wide variety of flavors and textures suitable for formal or informal dining; and which complement different foods. You can mix and match breads for their visual effect or for their taste alone; others change their nature radically when toasted. This section describes the basic characteristics of the better-known sandwich breads.

Soft cheeses like Brie and cottage cheese are not generally used in sandwiches. Brie is considered a dessert cheese, and cottage cheese is usually teamed with sliced fruit for dieters' salads. But this book includes recipes for sandwiches using both these cheeses, along with many other varieties of cheese. Some leave the choice of cheese up to you; others recommend a few cheeses with similar flavors, and still others call for one specific variety. This section also describes the basic flavor of most common cheeses to give you a starting point for your own adaptations.

The section of fish explores the various forms of seafood now available, and what to expect of them in sandwich making. Similarly, the last section on meat deals with the different types—especially lunch meats and "cold-cuts"—used for sandwiches; any of which can be used singly or in combination (as detailed later in this book) to prepare a fast but hearty repast.

Bread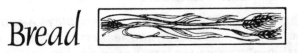

The pillar of every sandwich is its bread. Good bread won't guarantee you a great sandwich by any means, but you can't make a first-rate sandwich without good-quality bread. Fortunately, bread making in this country has recently undergone something of a renaissance, and there are plenty of excellent breads around—and even more for those who like to bake their own.

Although some people think of bread as calorie-packed ballast, two slices of whole wheat bread contain only 120 calories (far less than a four-ounce serving of chicken or even the leanest beef), as well as numerous vitamins, minerals, and rich fibers. Fresh, well-made bread is also deliciously satisfying in its own right, and complements an enormous range of foods. It's not called the staff of life for nothing.

The most commonly used bread in America today is good old white bread, made from refined wheat flour, which has had the bran removed. White bread comes in many different styles, of course; some are quite rich in taste and texture and others are less so. Oddly enough, bread made from "enriched" flour is usually less nourishing than that made from regular whole grain flour.

Nearly all commercial breads have at least some wheat flour in them, since that's the only type of flour that will enable a loaf to rise properly. **Whole wheat** bread is made, not surprisingly, from whole wheat flour, which uses the entire grain, bran included. **Rye** bread is made either partially or (rarely) entirely from rye flour, while **pumpernickel**—a dark, sourish bread—is made from whole, coarsely ground rye. **Sourdough** bread uses a sour fermenting batter as a leavener (unlike most breads, which use yeast) and is slightly moist, with a characteristically tangy taste. **Boston brown** bread is a rich, moist, rather sweet bread made from rye meal, cornmeal, graham flour, and molasses, among other ingredients. **Pita** bread is a soft, flat, round wheat bread whose two layers can be easily split at one end to hold fillings as securely as a mother kangaroo holds her joey. **Corn** bread is made with cornmeal and has a rich, crunchy texture. **Date** bread, **banana** bread, **raisin** bread, and other fruit-type breads usually contain some molasses, honey, and/or brown sugar along with the fruit and are excellent for sandwiches with sweet, fruity fillings.

Finally, no bread is as good as your own, and there's no better place to start making the perfect sandwich than by baking your own bread.

Cheese

Cheese is the star ingredient of many sandwiches and plays a supporting role in many more. This is not surprising, either: it has had a long and loving relationship with bread, as well as various meats and vegetables; and it comes in a wide variety of wonderfully subtle tastes and textures. It's also rich in protein and important minerals, particularly calcium and phosphorus.

Cheese is made from the pressed curd of milk, usually cow's milk, but sometimes goat's or ewe's. Most cheeses are solidified with rennin, an enzyme produced from the inner lining of animal intestines, but there are rennetless cheeses available at health food stores and certain grocery stores for orthodox vegetarians and those on kosher diets.

While certain cheeses are similar enough to be used interchangeably in sandwiches—Camembert and Brie, for example, or American and milk Cheddar—substituting something like Roquefort in a recipe calling for Muenster may result in something unusual, to say the least. Furthermore, some cheeses melt more easily than others and are thus especially appropriate for hot sandwiches. Among the more meltable are Gruyére, Muenster, Provolone, American, Swiss, and Cheddar. But watch out that you don't overcook them—they can get tough and leathery on the outside and have a trick of decomposing, with the fat separating from the rest of the cheese.

Two special subcategories of cheese, cottage and cream, deserve special mention, mainly because of their ability to mix with other foods to form tasty fillings. Even in De Gouy's day cottage cheese, the dieter's friend, was a familiar standby of the sandwich maker, in part because of its versatility. It could, he noted, "be made sweet with minced preserved fruits, dates, honey and fruit juices, or transformed into a spicy devilled type of filling by combining with olives, anchovies, pickles, mustard, minced chives and parsley, watercress, etc."

Cream cheese has a similarly adaptable nature, combining well with a wide range of fruits and vegetables, jellies and jams, nuts, and assorted flavorings. To make it easier to spread, just add a drop of milk or cream, though there is also a commercial brand of whipped cream cheese available that is much easier to spread than the regular kind.

The following list of cheeses is by no means comprehensive, but it does cover the more commonly used varieties, especially those appropriate for sandwiches.

American—A smooth, mild relative of Cheddar, ranging from white to yellow in color.

Bleu (Blue)—A pungent, semisoft white cheese with blue veins of mold running through it. Made from cow's milk and often used in sauces and dressings.

Brie—A soft, creamy, mold-ripened whole milk cheese with a creamy yellow interior and a subtle flavor ranging from mild to slightly pungent.

Camembert—Similar to Brie, but usually milder.

Cheddar—A smooth, fairly hard cheese ranging from mild to pungent in taste and from creamy white to dark yellow in color.

Cottage—A soft, mild, moist, low-calorie white cheese made from skim milk.

Cream—A soft, very mild white cheese, unripened and easy to spread.

Edam—A mild yellow Dutch cheese, often pressed into balls and coated with red paraffin.

Gouda—A mild, medium-textured, pale-yellow cheese made from either whole or partially skimmed milk and often covered with red paraffin.

Gruyére—A rather pungent, pale yellow, firm-textured cheese made from whole milk; may or may not have holes.

Jarlsberg—A smooth, fairly hard yellow cheese with a slightly sweet, nutty taste, an elastic texture, and round holes. Similar to Swiss.

Liederkranz—The trademark for a rather pungent, soft, surface-ripened cheese with a pale yellowish-brown color.

Muenster—A semisoft cheese with a creamy yellow interior and a pale gold surface; ranges from rather bland to fairly sharp in flavor, depending on the amount of curing time.

Neufchâtel—A French cream cheese that is low in butterfat.

Parmesan—A very hard, pungent, salty-tasting cheese that is grated and used for cooking.

Pasteurized process—A blend of aged and fresh cheeses which are shredded, mixed, and finally pasteurized. Melts easily and often has flavored materials added to it.

Provolone—A firm, off-white cheese whose flavor ranges from mild to fairly sharp.

Roquefort—A very pungent, blue-veined white cheese with a semisoft, crumbly texture. Made from goat's and ewe's milk and often used in sauces and dressing; similar to Bleu.

Swiss (Emmenthal)—A smooth, elastic-textured yellow cheese with round holes and a vaguely sharp, nutty flavor. Similar to Jarlsberg.

Fish

Most of us aren't likely to haul out the tackle box every time a recipe calls for seafood, so we have to rely on commercial fare. Fortunately, most seafood packaged in cans—anchovies, herring (kippered or pickled or creamed), salmon, sardines, tuna, shrimp, and crabmeat—is perfectly acceptable as sandwich components (but always check crabmeat carefully for fragments of shell). Sardines come packed in oil, or in a mustard or tomato sauce. Tuna is packed in either oil—usually vegetable oil, though some imported tuna comes in olive oil—or spring water. Don't forget to check your grocery shelves for other seafood specialties such as lobster or anchovy paste.

Crabmeat, lobster, and shrimp can be purchased fresh, frozen, or pre-cooked. Remember, though, that pre-cooked seafood tends to be overcooked—and therefore tough. In order to be at their best, "fresh" lobsters and crabs must be alive and wriggling when you buy them. Shrimps are offered in a variety of sizes, from the very small baby shrimp to jumbo shrimps two to three inches in length. There's nothing like biting into a shrimp salad made with enormous, juicy shrimp. But if a sandwich calls for a fine, paste-like filling, then we recommend using the smallest size you can find. Keep in mind how you intend to use your shrimp before you buy.

Freshwater and saltwater fish are available in most parts of the country in either fresh or frozen form. For a refreshing sandwich on a hot summer day, consider using flaked fish fillets in aspics. Most seafoods may also be fried with breadcrumbs and enjoyed on a roll, either plain or with cheese and/or tomato sauce.

When buying fresh seafood of any species, be sure it has been properly refrigerated or stored on ice. Plan on using it as soon as you return home; if you can't, put it in the deep freeze. Unfrozen fish may be stored in the refrigerator overnight, but no longer. After cooking, store it in the refrigerator for only a few more days, as it will lose flavor rather quickly.

Two types of fish deserve special—and honorable—mention. Smoked salmon, also known as lox, is usually considered an appetizer but is wonderful in thin slices on bread or bagels. Lox is available in salted and unsalted forms. The best is shipped from Nova Scotia and so, most higher grades are referred to as Nova Scotia lox. Whitefish, with its rich, characteristically oily meat, is also frequently used in salad and sandwiches, and is often sliced especially for sandwich purposes.

Meat

The meats used in sandwiches are a wonderfully varied lot. They come in all styles and manners of packaging; some are smoked, some are corned (salted or preserved in brine), some are pickled, and some are spiced; others are sold fresh or cured and uncooked in cans and jars. Most are available already sliced, and many can be sliced to order. Don't forget that the thickness can make a significant difference in the taste of your sandwich.

While some luncheon meats are pretty straightforward—roast beef, for example—others may vary considerably from store to store and region to region, particularly since many are mixtures of several different types of meat. If you're curious about a particular luncheon meat, ask your grocer. He should be happy to tell you just what it is he's slicing for you.

Even something as seemingly clear-cut as ham comes in a wide range of styles and can be purchased fresh, canned, or already cooked and sliced. While much of the ham sold as sandwich meat is just plain generic **ham,** honest and flavorful but without any particularly distinguished characteristics, there are a number of special varieties worth knowing about, especially given the number of recipes calling for sliced ham in this book.

Virginia ham is a firm, salty-flavored ham, available both uncooked (as a whole ham) and cooked and sliced. **Smithfield** ham is a special type of Virginia ham with an extremely salty, smoky flavor, a firm texture, and a mahogany color. It's made from peanut-fed hogs, and is cured, treated, and smoked in the town of Smithfield, Virginia. **Prosciutto** generally refers to the wonderfully seasoned, salt-cured, air-dried, uncooked ham of Parma, Italy; the term "prosciutto" is just an Italian word for ham. Prosciutto is traditionally sliced paper thin, and because of its intense, salty flavor, a little goes a pretty long way. **Capicola** is a rather lean Italian ham spiced with paprika. **Westphalian** ham is an uncooked, salty, reddish-brown German ham similar to prosciutto. **Irish** ham comes in several styles, most of which share a unique smoky flavor that comes from the peat-fire smoke with which they're cured. **York** ham has a mild flavor and delicate pink color.

The flavor of many sandwich meats, including bologna, salami, and pepperoni, is often enhanced by frying them lightly in a pan with no grease or oil. And while most people fry their bacon, it tends to be less greasy when boiled—an important consideration for sandwich making. Finally, many of the sandwich meats sold at delicatessens and the like contain bits of olives, pimientos, bacon, or other seasonings.

For those who have wondered about some of the generic luncheon meats they've been buying, here are some rather broad definitions. **Pastrami** is a highly seasoned smoked cut of beef (usually from the breast or shoulder) while **corned beef** is simply beef that has been preserved in brine. **Bologna** is a seasoned, smoked sausage made from mixed meats (often pork and beef), and **salami** is a highly spiced and salted sausage, again of mixed meats (often beef and pork), which comes in hard, soft, and kosher (no pork) styles. **Tongue** is usually that of a cow or ox and can be purchased fresh, pickled, corned, or smoked.

PART 2

Fine Tuning the Sandwich

Condiments

As with any other area of cooking, sandwiches can be as subtle as you choose to make them. All the various herbs, spices, and sauces employed in haute cuisine can help your sandwich become something of a gourmet meal in itself. It may not require too much finesse to assemble an ordinary ham-and-cheese sandwich, but the more sophisticated recipes demand a keen attention to detail. A key spice or dressing may not seem all that important, but its absence can mean the difference between the pleasantly palatable and the downright scrumptious.

This chapter includes a rundown of herbs and seasonings, recipes for sauces, dressing, and suggested garnishes, along with the more conventional sandwich condiments. For some recipes, the listed spices are essential to the sandwich's success; in other cases, they are simply suggestions. This chapter also lists the most commonly-used herbs and spices and what foods they complement.

Sauces are not generally associated with sandwiches, but many of De Gouy's creations use different sauces to their (and your) advantage. Although we provide recipes for salad dressings, don't be reluctant to try out your own favorite dressing (homemade or commercial) on your next appropriate sandwich.

Garnishes are usually thought of as those inedible spots of color on the side of the plate. In reality, though, a garnish should be carefully chosen to complement the sandwich's taste. Relishes, for example, are excellent if spread directly on the sandwich or, depending on the selection, parked on the side as free-form garnishes.

Similarly, you have many options available besides the standard sweet or unsalted butters. A seasoned or compounded butter will flavor a sandwich delicately without overpowering it, and the side selection of butters included here include one for almost any sandwich combination. Although classified as a condiment here, butter can also be delicious when used alone on bread, to form a lighter kind of sandwich.

Mustard and mayonnaise are two condiments familiar to nearly everyone, but there are important differences among the various kinds. Besides explaining the characteristics of the various mustards, we have given basic recipes for making your own mayonnaise and various tantalizing variations.

Here, then, are a number of possibilities and extra touches that can act as springboards for even more personal and exotic creations of your own.

Dressings and Sauces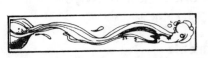

The following dressings and sauces are included to supplement De Gouy's original recipes, and most of them are intentionally basic. Depending on how you plan to use a dressing or sauce, certain herbs and spices can make an amazing difference. They may be added to vinaigrette sauce to subtly change the flavor of a sandwich or added to white sauce to produce a variety of changes capable of complimenting many ingredients. We suggest you consult the section dealing with herbs and spices and use them as a point of departure for your own ideas.

French Dressing or Vinaigrette Sauce

3 or 4 parts oil to 1 part vinegar. Salt and pepper to taste. Shake well before using.

Russian Dressing

2 parts mayonnaise, 1 part ketchup, and 1 part pickle relish. Mix well.

Brown Sauce

2 Tbs. butter
2 Tbs. flour
1 cup bouillon
pepper

Melt the butter in a saucepan and stir in the flour until it forms a paste. Stir in the bouillon and heat. Season with pepper.

Cheese Sauce

½ cup **white sauce**
½ cup grated cheese
paprika
pepper
¼ tsp. dry mustard

When the white sauce is smooth and hot, stir in the grated cheese until it melts. Add the dry mustard and season to taste with the pepper and paprika.

Mushroom Sauce

¼ lb. mushrooms
2 Tbs. butter
brown sauce

Slice the mushrooms and sauté them in the butter. Remove mushrooms from the pan and stir the brown sauce in with the pan drippings from the mushrooms. Heat and serve.

Welsh Rarebit

1 lb. Cheddar cheese
1 Tbs. butter
1 cup beer
1 tsp. Worcestershire sauce

Melt the butter in a double broiler and stir in the beer. When the beer is warm, stir in the cheese. Stir frequently until melted and season with the Worcestershire sauce.

Variations:

1. Sausage such as pepperoni may be chopped and added to the cheese as it is melting.
2. Canned cheese soup may be purchased and used for a quicker version. Heat the soup according to the instructions on the can, then pour in the beer and add the Worcestershire sauce.

White Sauce

2 Tbs. butter
2 Tbs. flour
1 cup milk

In a saucepan, melt the butter and stir in the flour. When it is the consistency of a smooth paste, slowly stir in the milk. Heat but do not boil. Herbs (such as celery flakes or dill) may be added to this sauce.

Variation:

1. Egg Sauce. Proceed as above but add two chopped, hard-boiled eggs to the sauce after milk is stirred in.

Garnishes

If you're cooking for yourself, chances are you're not going to bother much with garnishes. But if you're making a sandwich for someone else, a sprig of parsley or a sculpted radish is a compliment in every sense of the word—like serving wine in a wine glass instead of a coffee mug. Even something as casual as a sandwich ought to be pleasing to the eye as well as the palate, but don't forget that the garnish should complement the taste of the sandwich, too. We've left De Gouy's suggested garnishes in a number of the recipes that follow. The list below contains a wide selection of other garnishes in which you'll find something suitable for almost any occasion or sandwich combination. Some of the garnishes, such as horseradish sauce and relishes, are also excellent on the sandwiches themselves.

Apples—Cubed, sliced, in rings, rolled in paprika, minced parsley, chives, or curry powder.

Cheese—Cubed, sliced, rolled into small balls, then rolled in paprika, parsley, curry powder, saffron, nuts, or chives.

Dill Pickles—Cubed, sliced, cut fanlike, in sticks or in cups, and filled with cottage cheese or mayonnaise.

Green Pepper—In cups, sliced in rings, or chopped.

Hard-Boiled Eggs—Chopped, sliced, quartered, halved, sieved, then mixed with parsley, chives, chopped dill, or capers.

Horseradish—Plain or mixed with prepared mustard or dressing, fresh or shredded, in small balls, mixed with cottage cheese.

Lemon—Sliced thin, dipped in paprika or minced parsley or chives, or in cups filled with dressing.

Lettuce—Shredded, crisp leaves, or in cups with dressing.

Mint—Especially for lamb sandwiches; fresh mint leaves, mint jelly cubes.

Olives—Black, green, ripe, or stuffed, scooped, filled with cottage cheese or horseradish.

Parsley—Fresh and crisp, minced, sprig, or bunches.

Pimiento—Sliced, chopped, or in cups filled with minced onion.

Radishes—Sliced, dressed with mayonnaise, or scooped and filled with horseradish, mayonnaise, or cheese.

Relishes—Such as tomato and onion, pickled beets, spiced green beans, curried tomato relish, chow-chow, pickled cucumbers and onion slices, cabbage relish, cole slaw, pickled cauliflowers. Many of these are also excellent on the sandwich itself.

Tomatoes—Ripe or green, sliced, quartered, or halved and filled with chopped nuts, creamed cheese with nuts, olives, or fruit.

Watercress—Crisp and green, either sprigs or a generous bunch.

Herbs and Spices

If you've ever tasted fresh basil on a ripe tomato, or cinammon in a cup of freshly brewed coffee, you know the difference that herbs and spices can make. Properly used, they can add entire new dimensions to foods, bringing out subtleties of flavor that would otherwise remain hidden.

Herbs can be bought fresh, dried, and ground, but if it's at all possible you should try to grow your own. Fresh herbs have a good deal more flavor and zip than their dried counterparts, though dried herbs certainly do the trick. Since they shouldn't just be tossed on indiscriminately, here is a list of some of the more commonly used herbs and spices with the foods they've been found to complement best.

Herbs
Basil: tomatoes, seafood.

Celery seeds or flakes: seafood salads, potatoes, certain sauces.

Chives: eggs, vegetables, certain sauces.

Dill: salmon, sour cream, sauces, eggs.

Garlic (or garlic powder): lamb, other meats.

Marjoram: eggs, greens, meats, sauces.

Oregano: tomatoes, other vegetables, seafood salads.

Parsley: eggs, fish, poultry, certain sauces; as a garnish when fresh.

Rosemary: meats, fish, poultry, vegetables.

Tarragon: poultry, salads, eggs, seafoods.

Thyme: salads, meats, fish, poultry, cheeses.

Spices

Caraway seeds: used in breads.

Cayenne: meat dishes and sauces—very hot and pungent.

Cinammon: fruits, certain meats.

Cloves: apples, ham, poultry.

Nutmeg: poultry, spinach, fruits.

Paprika: eggs, potatoes, salads, and as a garnish for sauces.

Pepper: meats, cheeses, eggs, vegetables.

Poppy seeds: used in breads.

Sesame seeds: used in breads.

Mayonnaise

While most people are content to get their mayonnaise from their grocer, aficionados swear by the homemade type, which is usually fresher, livelier, and more delicate to the taste. If you do buy your mayonnaise from a store, however, remember that **real** mayonnaise, which is made with eggs, spoils fairly quickly if not refrigerated; the same goes for the homemade kind. Imitation mayonnaise, which is not made with eggs, is much more resistant to spoilage and is thus particularly handy on a picnic. The following mayonnaises should keep for weeks if properly refrigerated.

Mayonnaise 1

¾ cup olive oil or vegetable oil
½ tsp. dry mustard
½ tsp. sugar
½ tsp. salt
few grains cayenne
1 egg yolk
1 Tbs. vinegar
1 Tbs. lemon juice

Mix well mustard, salt, sugar, and cayenne in a small deep bowl. Add the egg yolk and mix thoroughly. Stirring constantly, add the vinegar, then **very slowly** beat in the oil, making sure the mixture is perfectly smooth each time before adding more. Then stir in the lemon juice. (If you don't plan to use it the day you make it, add 1 tsp. hot water.)

Mayonnaise 2

1 egg
½ tsp. dry mustard
½ tsp. salt

1 Tbs. lemon juice
1 Tbs. vinegar
1½ cups olive oil or vegetable oil

Beat egg until thick, then beat in dry mustard, salt, lemon juice, and vinegar. Add oil very slowly, beating until thick and smooth each time before adding more.

Curry Mayonnaise

1 cup mayonnaise
1 tsp. curry powder
¼ tsp. ginger powder (optional)
small garlic clove, pressed (optional)

Combine the above ingredients and chill.

Mustard Mayonnaise

1 cup mayonnaise
1 Tbs. dry mustard

Combine the above ingredients and mix thoroughly.

Mustard

There are almost as many different types of mustard as there are foods that are complemented by them—which is to say quite a few. Mustard adds zing (there's no other word for it) to any number of sandwich-oriented foods, including ham, pastrami, numerous cheeses, various sausages, and more. As a nation, we've always been partial to the stuff, and in recent years the demand for more subtle and exotic varieties has resulted in a sizable increase in the number of mustards available to us.

Some of the finest mustards come from Dijon, the capital of Burgundy, and range in style from mild to quite pungent (and sometimes flavored with interesting herbs), with a beguiling tartness that comes from the addition of **verjuice,** the highly acidic juice of unripened grapes. Another famous French wine-making region, Bordeaux, also adds **must** (unfermented or partially fermented juice of grapes) to its fine sweet-and-sour mustards; in case you were wondering, that's where **must**ard got its name.

Some other good mustards on the market include:

Chinese—Same as English, and guaranteed to open up your sinuses.

Dusseldorf—A smooth, mildly spiced German mustard.

English (or Colman's)—A very hot mustard with nothing added to tone it down.

Grey-Poupon—An American version of the Grey-Poupon of Dijon: mild, subtle, and pleasant.

Savora—A smooth-textured, slightly sweet mustard from France.

Zatarin's Creole—A grainy, mildly spiced mustard from New Orleans.

Several other American brands are available in most supermarkets, and while they're not particularly exotic, they're often quite good with ham and other meats, adding the characteristic tanginess without overpowering everything else.

Seasoned and Compounded Butters

The following seasoned and compounded butters can do wonderful things for a sandwich. Like most seasonings, they complement and accentuate certain ingredients; they also add a moist and pervasive richness of flavor that dried herbs, for example, cannot. Keep stored in tightly sealed glass jars in the refrigerator.

For each of these butters proceed as follows: Add the listed ingredients to ¼ lb. of creamed butter.

Almond Butter—Work in 2 Tbs. blanched, ground almonds and a few drops lemon juice.

American Cheese Butter—Work in 2 Tbs. grated American cheese and a few drops Worcestershire sauce.

Anchovy Butter—Work in a few drops lemon juice, ½ tsp. anchovy paste, and ½ tsp. finely minced parsley.

Apple Sauce Butter—Work in 2 Tbs. apple sauce and 1 Tbs. ground nuts.

Apricot Butter—Work in 2 Tbs. cooked, sieved apricot (rather firm) and a few drops lemon juice.

Caviar Butter—Work in 1 Tbs. well-drained caviar, a few drops lemon juice, and ½ tsp. grated onion.

Chili Butter—Work in 3 Tbs. chili sauce and a few drops lemon juice.

Chive Butter—Work in 2 Tbs. finely minced chives and 1 tsp. grated onion.

Chutney Butter—Work in 1 generous Tbs. ground mustard chutney and a few drops Tabasco sauce.

Egg Yolk Butter—Work in 1 sieved, hard-boiled egg yolk, a sprinkle of onion powder, and 1 Tbs. finely minced parsley.

Garlic Butter—In a few drops of water or vinegar blanch a clove of garlic. Remove and dry and either mash or put through a garlic press. Work into the butter.

Green Pepper Butter—Work in 3 Tbs. grated, well-drained green pepper and a few drops lemon juice.

Herring Butter—Work in 1 Tbs. ground smoked herring, free of bones, and a few drops lemon juice.

Honey Butter—Work in 1 Tbs. honey and a few drops each lemon juice and Tabasco sauce.

Horseradish Butter—Work in 2 Tbs. well-drained horseradish and 1 Tbs. finely minced chives.

Jam Butter—Work in 2 Tbs. any kind of jam and a few drops lemon juice.

Jelly Butter—Work in 2 Tbs. any kind of jelly and a few drops lemon juice. If desired, 1 Tbs. ground nuts may be added.

Ketchup Butter—Work in 3 Tbs. ketchup and 2 tsp. grated onion.

Lemon Butter—Add 2 tsp. lemon juice to creamed butter and ½ tsp. grated lemon rind.

Liverwurst Butter—Work in 3 Tbs. mashed liverwurst and a few drops lemon juice or 1 tsp. grated onion.

Lobster Butter—Work in ½ cup cooked, ground lobster and a few drops lemon juice.

Molasses Butter—Work in 1 tsp. molasses and ¼ tsp. grated lemon or orange rind.

Mustard Butter—Work in 2 tsp. prepared mustard and a few drops lemon juice.

Nut Butter—Work in 2 Tbs. any kind of ground nut and ¼ tsp. grated orange rind.

Olive Pimiento Butter—Mix together 2 chopped pimientos and ¼ cup chopped, stuffed olives; let stand in the refrigerator overnight to mellow before using.

Orange Butter—Add 2 tsp. orange juice and ½ tsp. grated orange rind.

Paprika Butter—Work in 1 Tbs. paprika and a sprinkle of onion powder.

Parsley Butter—Work in 2 Tbs. finely minced parsley and a few drops Tabasco sauce or Worcestershire sauce.

Peanut Butter—Use plain or mixed with equal parts sweet, creamed butter and peanut butter.

Pimiento Butter—Work in 2 Tbs. finely chopped red pimientos well pressed to reduce liquid.

Pineapple-Ginger Butter—Work in 2 Tbs. canned, crushed, and well-drained pineapple with a few grains ginger powder.

Potted Meat Butter—Work in any kind of canned meat, such as deviled ham, using 2 generous Tbs., a few drops of lemon juice, and a sprinkle of onion powder.

Prune Butter—Work in 2 Tbs. cooked, sieved, rather stiff or firm prune pulp, and add ½ tsp. grated lemon rind.

Roquefort Cheese Butter—Work in 2 generous Tbs. of Roquefort cheese mashed with a few drops Worcestershire sauce.

Salmon Butter—Use fresh cooked, or smoked salmon. Work in 2 Tbs. salmon, ground or pounded to a paste, a few drops lemon juice and Worcestershire sauce.

Sardine Butter—Work in ¼ cup boned, skinned, and thoroughly drained canned sardines with ½ tsp. onion, ½ tsp. lemon juice, and a few drops Tabasco sauce.

Shrimp Butter—Work in 1½ Tbs. cooked, canned or fresh shrimp, ground or pounded to a paste, and a sprinkle of onion powder and lemon juice.

Tarragon Butter—Work in 2 or 3 finely chopped leaves fresh tarragon, and a few drops tarragon vinegar.

Vegetable Butter—Work in any kind of cold, cooked, ground green vegetable, a few drops lemon juice, 1 tsp. grated onion, and a few drops Tabasco sauce.

Watercress Butter—Work in 3 Tbs. finely minced watercress.

Fillings and Salads

The following fillings and salads can be used either by themselves or in combination with other ingredients. Most of the salads are somewhat basic by design, since they share the spotlight with numerous other ingredients in the suggested sandwich combinations that follow; don't be bashful about tinkering with them.

For those recipes calling for chopped nuts, try using a blender or a food processor; the latter can be used for chopping almost anything.

The combinations are listed in alphabetical order according to their main ingredient. Those combinations whose main ingredient is cheese can be found under either "Cheese" or the specific type of cheese called for, if there is one. Sauces and dressings are listed in bold face; the recipes for them can be found by checking the index.

American Cheese and Nut Filling

10 Tbs. grated American cheese
¼ cup coarsely chopped nuts
mayonnaise

To the American cheese add nuts and moisten with mayonnaise. Serve on rye bread. Makes one cup.

Apple Celery Salad

chopped apples
chopped celery hearts
chopped nuts (optional)

vinaigrette sauce or mayonnaise
lemon juice

Sprinkle the apples with lemon juice to keep them from browning. Combine equal parts apple and celery with either mayonnaise or vinaigrette sauce and chill. Add chopped nuts if desired.

Apricot Filling 1

½ lb. dried apricots
¾ cup granulated sugar
rind of ½ large orange
½ cup chopped seedless raisins
½ cup chopped nuts

Soak the apricots in cold water for 4 hours. Drain and chop. Add the sugar, the shredded orange rind, raisins, and nuts. Cook over gentle heat for an hour, stirring occasionally. Cool and chill. Makes two cups.

Apricot Filling 2

1 cup dried apricots
2 cups water
½ cup granulated sugar
3 Tbs. ground blanched almonds

Boil the apricots in the water with sugar for 10 minutes, then cover and simmer 15 to 20 minutes. Remove from the fire and sieve. Add the almonds and cool. When using, heat the amount desired and spread on toast. Makes one cup.

Avocado Filling

1 cup avocado pulp
2 tsp. lemon juice
½ tsp. onion powder
1 tsp. salt

Combine the avocado pulp, lemon juice, onion powder, and salt. Stir until smooth. Serve on rye bread. Makes one cup.

Baked Beans Horseradish Filling

1 cup cold baked beans
3 Tbs. drained horseradish
Worcestershire sauce

Using a blender or a sieve, make a paste from the baked beans and add the horseradish along with a few drops of the Worcestershire sauce. Mix well. Serve on toast. Makes one cup.

Bean Salad

2½ cups cooked beans (any kind)
¼ cup **vinaigrette sauce**

Drain and chill the beans. Combine with the vinaigrette sauce and let sit before using.

Beef Salad

thin slices cold cooked beef
hard-boiled eggs, chopped
vinaigrette sauce
parsley
chopped celery (optional)

Toss the beef, eggs, parsley, and celery together. Pour enough vinaigrette sauce over it to moisten the ingredients but not soak them. Chill.

Cabbage Salad

chopped or shredded cabbage
chopped carrots
chopped celery
small clove garlic or garlic powder
pepper
vinaigrette sauce

Combine the cabbage, carrots, and celery using 3 parts cabbage to 1 part each of carrots and celery. Pour vinaigrette sauce over this mixture and work in a pressed clove of garlic or sprinkle with garlic powder. Season with pepper to taste.
Variation:
1. Mix with mayonnaise instead of vinaigrette sauce.

Carrot Filling

1 cup grated raw carrot
5 Tbs. mayonnaise
1 tsp. salt
few grains pepper
½ cup chopped nuts
1 Tbs. lemon juice
few drops Worcestershire sauce

Mix together thoroughly the above ingredients. Store in the refrigerator until using. Serve on graham bread. Makes 1½ cups.

Celery Salad

1 medium-sized bunch celery
1 cup **vinaigrette sauce**

chopped green onion or chives

Using only the inner stalks, the heart, and the small leaves of the celery, cut into fairly small pieces and soak in vinaigrette sauce for several hours. Before using, sprinkle with chopped green onion or chives.

Cheese, Dried Beef, and Tomatoes

½ lb. dried beef, finely chopped
¼ lb. grated American, Edam, or Cheddar cheese
1 pt. tomato soup

Mix the dried beef, American cheese, and tomato soup together and cook until the mixture thickens. When cold, use as a filling. Garnish with an olive and a slice of green pepper. Keeps well in the refrigerator.

Cheese and Green Pepper Filling

grated American, Edam, or Cheddar cheese
minced green pepper
chopped stuffed olives
mayonnaise

Combine equal parts of grated cheese, green pepper, and olives. Blend with mayonnaise.

Cheese and Spinach Filling

American, Edam, or Cheddar cheese
uncooked spinach
lemon juice
mayonnaise

Moisten equal parts of ground cheese and chopped or ground spinach with lemon juice and mayonnaise.

Chicken Salad 1

1 cup chopped chicken
½ cup chopped celery
1 Tbs. chopped onions (optional)
salt and pepper
mayonnaise

To prepare this salad you may use leftover chicken, canned chicken, or freshly poached chicken. Combine chicken, celery, and onions evenly in mixing bowl. Stir in mayonnaise and salt and pepper according to taste.
Variations:

1. Stir in 2 Tbs. chopped pimientos.
2. Before stirring in mayonnaise add ½ cup chopped black olives.
3. Use ½ cup chopped, peeled apples and ¼ cup chopped walnuts.
4. Add ½ cup seedless green grapes cut in halves.

Chicken Salad 2

½ cup cold cooked chicken
3 olives
½ green pepper
1½ tsp. chili sauce
3 Tbs. mayonnaise
few drops Worcestershire sauce
2 hard-boiled eggs

Put the chicken, olives, green pepper, and eggs through a food chopper. Add the chili sauce and mayonnaise to moisten, then add a few drops Worcestershire sauce. Mix well. Serve on toast. Makes 1¼ cups.

Chicken Salad 3

1 cup finely chopped cold cooked chicken
½ cup finely chopped nuts
mustard mayonnaise

Combine the chicken with the nuts. (Do not grind the chicken; it should be chopped.) Mix the chicken and nuts with mustard mayonnaise. Serve on graham bread. Makes 1½ cups.

Cole Slaw

small head of cabbage
½ cup mayonnaise
½ cup sour cream
1 Tbs. lemon juice
1 Tbs. sugar
1 tsp. dry mustard
salt and pepper

Mix all the ingredients together and pour over shredded cabbage that has been soaking in salt water for 1 hour. Mix well and let stand before using.

Variation:

1. Red Cole Slaw. Red cabbage may be substituted for some or all of the cabbage.

Corned Beef Hash

1½ cups cooked meat
½ cup cubed cooked potatoes
1 medium onion
salt and pepper
celery seed

Grind the meat, potatoes, and onion together. Add salt, pepper, and celery seed to taste. Cook in a skillet over medium heat in butter or fat until a crust starts to form on one side. Turn it over and continue to cook, stirring occasionally. Shortly before it is done, pat into a flat cake. Cooking time should be about 20 minutes.

Cottage Cheese Filling
1 cup sieved cottage cheese
2 Tbs. minced chives
2 Tbs. grated onion
2 Tbs. minced parsley
2 Tbs. minced green olives
salt and white pepper

Mix together all of the above ingredients and season to taste with salt and pepper. Store in the refrigerator, as this mixture does not keep very long. Makes 1½ cups.

Variation:

1. Substitute cream cheese for the cottage cheese and proceed as above.

Cottage Cheese and Carrot Filling
cottage cheese
grated raw carrot
1 tsp. sweet pickles, finely chopped
salt and pepper

To 3 parts cottage cheese, add 1 part carrot and the sweet pickles. Season to taste with salt and pepper.

Variation:

1. Chopped nuts may be substituted for sweet pickles.

Cottage Cheese and Cherry Preserves Filling
cottage cheese
cherry preserves
Worcestershire sauce
salt and pepper

Combine and mix thoroughly equal parts of cottage cheese and well-drained, chopped cherry preserves. Season to taste with a few drops Worcestershire sauce, salt, and pepper.

Cottage Cheese and Cinnamon Filling
cottage cheese
cinnamon
salt and pepper
sugar

After putting cottage cheese through a sieve, season highly with cinnamon, salt and pepper, and a little sugar to taste.

Cottage Cheese, Honey, and Nuts Filling
cottage cheese
honey
chopped nuts (any kind)

Mix together thoroughly equal parts cottage cheese, honey, and chopped nuts.

Cottage Cheese and Olive Filling
1 cup cottage cheese
½ tsp. Worcestershire sauce
2 Tbs. chili sauce
½ cup chopped ripe olives
salt and white pepper

Put the cottage cheese through a sieve. To it add the Worcestershire sauce, chili sauce, and olives. Season to taste with salt and white pepper.

Cottage Cheese and Raisin Filling
¼ cup well-drained cottage cheese
2 crushed saltines or Graham crackers
1 Tbs. mayonnaise
¼ cup seedless raisins, chopped very fine

To the cup of well-drained, sieved cottage cheese add the crackers, mayonnaise, and raisins. Mix thoroughly.

Crabmeat Salad
1 cup crabmeat
½ cup finely chopped celery
1½ Tbs. grated onion
½ cup mayonnaise

Flake the crabmeat and add all the ingredients. Mix well. Serve on toast. Makes 2½ cups.
Variations:
1. Seafood such as lobster, shrimp, tuna, or salmon may be used instead of crabmeat.
2. Chicken, veal, or pork may be substituted for the crabmeat.

Cream Cheese and Almond Filling
1 lb. cream cheese
¼ cup pickle relish
½ cup ground blanched almonds
¼ cup celery leaves, ground
salt and pepper
paprika

Worcestershire sauce

Combine all of the above ingredients until smooth. You may put it through a food blender to ensure smoothness. This spread refrigerates well.

Cream Cheese and Apricot Filling
cream cheese
stewed or canned apricots
mayonnaise
nuts (optional)

Mix together equal parts cream cheese and apricot pulp (made by pressing through a sieve the stewed or canned apricots which have been thoroughly drained). Add mayonnaise to taste and chopped nuts if desired.

Cream Cheese and Banana Filling
3 oz. cream cheese
1 large banana
1 tsp. lemon juice
salt

Sieve the banana with lemon juice to prevent darkening. Also sieve the cream cheese, and then sieve the banana and the cream cheese together. Add salt to taste. Serve on date nut bread or Boston brown bread. This does not keep long. Makes one cup.

Cream Cheese and Beets Filling
cream cheese
cooked beets

Combine equal parts cream cheese and cooked beets; mix thoroughly.

Cream Cheese and Caraway Seed Filling
¼ lb. cream cheese
¼ lb. butter
½ tsp. caraway seeds
½ tsp. grated onions
1½ Tbs. heavy cream
salt and pepper

Blend all the above ingredients until smooth and season to taste with salt and pepper.

Cream Cheese and Celery Filling
1 lb. cream cheese
1 cup finely chopped celery

Blend the cream cheese and celery together.

Cream Cheese, Celery, and Cherry Filling

1 lb. cream cheese
⅔ cup chopped celery
⅔ cup chopped canned cherries

To the cream cheese add the chopped celery and cherries (making sure that the cherries have been well drained).

Variations:
1. Substitute chopped dates for cherries.
2. Substitute chopped figs for cherries.

Cream Cheese, Chives, and Pineapple Filling

6 oz. cream cheese
2 or 3 Tbs. finely minced chives
2 Tbs. mayonnaise
1 cup well-drained canned crushed pineapple

Cream the cream cheese and blend with the chives, mayonnaise, and pineapple. This mixture keeps well and is especially good on raisin bread. Makes two cups.

Cream Cheese, Cottage Cheese, and Nuts Filling

cream cheese
cottage cheese, well-drained and sieved
chopped nuts (any kind)
evaporated milk
salt and pepper
Worcestershire sauce

Combine in equal parts the cream cheese, cottage cheese, and chopped nuts. Add enough of the evaporated milk to make the mixture a spreadable consistency. Season to taste with salt, pepper, and a few drops Worcestershire sauce. Very good on corn bread.

Cream Cheese and Honey Filling

3 oz. cream cheese
½ cup honey
3 Tbs. blanched ground almonds

Blend the above ingredients together and serve on rye, Boston brown, or graham bread. Makes one cup and keeps three to four weeks.

Cream Cheese and Horseradish Filling

cream cheese
horseradish
salt and pepper

Combine and blend well equal parts cream cheese and horseradish. Salt and pepper to taste.

Cream Cheese, Horseradish, and Nut Filling

cream cheese
horseradish
chopped nuts (any kind)

Combine and blend thoroughly the cream cheese, horseradish, and chopped nuts.

Cream Cheese, Pimiento, and Walnut Filling

cream cheese
minced pimiento
chopped walnuts

Combine and blend well equal parts cream cheese, pimientos, and walnuts.

Cream Cheese and Pineapple Filling

cream cheese
shredded pineapple

Combine and blend thoroughly cream cheese and shredded pineapple (if canned, make sure it is well drained).

Cream Cheese and Watercress Filling

cream cheese
finely minced watercress
salt and pepper
Worcestershire sauce

Combine equal parts cream cheese and watercress. Season to taste with salt and pepper and a dash of Worcestershire sauce.

Cream Cheese, Watercress, and Apple Butter Filling

cream cheese
apple butter
finely minced watercress
salt and pepper

Combine equal parts cream cheese, apple butter, and watercress. Season to taste with salt and pepper.

Variations:

1. Substitute peanut butter for the apple butter.
2. Substitute butter for the apple butter.

Creamed Tuna

tuna fish (drained)

white sauce
chicken stock or bouillon (optional)
pepper

When preparing the white sauce for this recipe, half of the milk may be eliminated and chicken stock or bouillon used in its place. Stir in the tuna fish and season with pepper. Serve hot or cold.

Variations:

1. Creamed Chicken. Substitute finely chopped or shredded chicken for the tuna fish. Season with savory.

2. Creamed Crabmeat. Substitute crabmeat for the tuna fish. Season with celery seeds and pepper.

Cucumber Salad
cucumber
vinaigrette sauce
salt and pepper

Peel the cucumber and cut into thin slices. Cover with vinaigrette sauce and soak for several hours until they are wilted. Season with salt and pepper. May be enjoyed on toasted bread or combined with cheeses or fish for a special taste.

Deviled Cheese Filling
1 cup grated cheese (any kind of hard grating cheese)
¼ tsp. salt
1 tsp. paprika
½ tsp. Worcestershire sauce
½ tsp. vinegar
1 tsp. peanut butter
½ (or more) tsp. prepared mustard
a few grains cayenne

Combine and blend thoroughly. Spread between 2 slices of any kind of bread.

Deviled Eggs
hard-boiled egg
mayonnaise
salt
paprika
dry mustard

Remove the yolks and mash with a little mayonnaise. Season with salt and paprika. Add a little dry mustard. Mash the egg whites back into the yolks for a sandwich spread.

Variation:

1. Curried Eggs. Proceed as above but substitute heavy cream for the mayonnaise, adding just enough to mash smoothly, and season with curry powder to taste. Chopped almonds may be added.

Dried Beef and American Cheese Filling

½ cup dried beef
½ cup ground American cheese
ketchup
few grains dry mustard

Blend the beef and cheese together and moisten with a little ketchup. Add the dry mustard and mix thoroughly. Makes one cup.

Dried Beef Country Style

¼ lb. dried beef
¼ lb. American cheese
⅓ cup tomato sauce
1 egg
pepper

Put the cheese and beef through a food chopper. Mix with the tomato sauce and cook in a double boiler until heated and well blended. Remove from heat and add a well-beaten egg and a little pepper. Cool. This mixture keeps well for several weeks. Makes 1¼ cups.

Dried Beef and Horseradish Filling

1 cup dried beef
vinaigrette sauce
4 Tbs. well-drained horseradish

To the ground dried beef, add enough vinaigrette sauce to moisten and add horseradish. Serve on pumpernickel or Boston brown bread. Makes one cup and lasts about three weeks.

Dried Beef and Peanut Butter Filling

1 cup peanut butter
½ dried beef
½ cup chili sauce
2 Tbs. minced parsley

Scald, drain, and then grind the dried beef. Mix with peanut butter, chili sauce, and parsley. Serve on plain or toasted bread. This will make two cups and will keep for several weeks.

Egg Mayonnaise Filling

6 hard-boiled eggs
salt

paprika
mayonnaise

Finely chop the egg whites and press the yolks through a potato ricer. Mix yolks and whites together and moisten with mayonnaise. Season with salt and paprika. Serve on graham bread. Makes one cup and keeps for one week.

Egg Salad
4 hard-boiled eggs
½ cup chopped celery
mayonnaise
salt and pepper

Chop the eggs to the desired consistency (some prefer the eggs finely chopped, almost mashed, while others prefer large chunks of egg in their salad). Add celery and stir in mayonnaise. Salt and pepper to taste. Makes one cup.

Variations:

1. Substitute sour cream for mayonnaise.
2. Add chopped pimiento.
3. Add chopped onion and green pepper.
4. Add chopped marinated artichoke hearts.

Far East Filling
2 large white onions, minced
½ cup celery, minced
½ green pepper, minced
small clove garlic (optional)
3 Tbs. cooking oil
½ tsp. curry powder
2 cans sardines
¼ cup sweet pickles, minced
8 pitted green olives, minced
6 hard-boiled eggs, minced
mayonnaise
lemon juice
Tabasco sauce
salt and pepper

Cook the onions, peppers, celery, and garlic together in the cooking oil until they soften, stirring frequently. Season with the salt, pepper, and curry powder (more curry may be added if desired). Drain the oil from the sardines and mash thoroughly. Add the sardines to the cooked vegetables with the sweet pickles, olives, and hard-boiled eggs. Moisten with a little mayonnaise, lemon juice, and Tabasco sauce. Mix together well and store in a jar in the refrigerator. Keeps for months.

Fig and Date Filling
dried figs
dates
1 tsp. lemon juice

Put enough figs and dates through the food chopper to obtain 1 cup of each. Add enough cold water to barely cover them in a pan and simmer to form a paste. Add the lemon juice and cool. Serve on thin slices of nut bread. This recipe makes two cups, and keeps for several weeks.

Fish Roe Mayonnaise Filling
2½ to 3 Tbs. cooked or smoked fish roe
mayonnaise
1 tsp. grated onion

Grind the fish roe and moisten with mayonnaise. Add to this the grated onion. Serve on toast with peanut butter. This makes one serving and should be used right away.

Ginger Date Filling
½ cup finely chopped dates
½ cup chopped walnuts
¼ cup chopped preserved ginger
lemon juice or ginger syrup

Mix the dates, walnuts, and ginger together. Moisten with lemon juice or ginger syrup. Blend thoroughly. Serve on graham bread spread with peanut butter. Makes 1½ cups and keeps two to three weeks.

Green Bean Salad
cooked green beans
vinaigrette sauce
chopped onions or chives (optional)

Drain the green beans and cover them with vinaigrette sauce. Let chill for a few hours and add onions if desired.

Variations:

1. Thinly sliced mushrooms may be added before chilling.
2. Crisp bacon may be crumbled and added with the onions.

Ham, Giblets, and Egg Filling
giblets from 1 chicken
½ cup cooked ham
1 hard-boiled egg
2 Tbs. mayonnaise or cream
1 Tbs. grated onion
½ tsp. Worcestershire sauce
1 Tbs. ketchup
salt and pepper

Clean and cook the chicken giblets in boiling salted water until tender. Drain and put through a food chopper with the ham and hard-boiled egg. Blend in the mayonnaise or cream, the onion, Worcestershire sauce, and ketchup, and season with salt and pepper to taste. Serve on toast. This makes one cup and keeps for three or four weeks.

Ham and Jelly Filling

1 cup finely chopped or ground ham
½ cup currant jelly
½ cup butter
1 tsp. paprika

Cream the butter and mix with the ham, jelly, and paprika. Serve on white or whole wheat bread. Makes two cups and keeps two weeks.

Ham and Mayonnaise Filling

1 ¼ cups ground ham
6 Tbs. mayonnaise
3 Tbs. finely chopped chutney
1 ½ Tbs. chutney syrup

Mix together thoroughly the ham, mayonnaise, chutney, and chutney syrup. Serve on white or Boston brown bread. Makes one cup and keeps for weeks.

Ham and Raw Vegetable Filling

½ cup ground ham
raw vegetables (such as carrots, onions, green pepper)
mayonnaise
salt and pepper

Grind or grate enough raw vegetables to make ½ cup. Add the ham, moisten with mayonnaise, and blend together well. Season to taste with salt and pepper. Serve on rye bread. Keeps a few days and makes one cup.

Ham Salad

2 ½ cups cubed ham
½ cup chopped celery
½ cup chopped green onion
mustard mayonnaise

Combine all the ingredients and blend with mustard mayonnaise

Ham and Walnut Filling

1 cup ground ham
½ cup chopped walnuts
1 Tbs. prepared mustard
4 Tbs. mayonnaise or cream
salt and pepper
few drops Tabasco sauce

Combine and mix thoroughly the above ingredients. Season to taste with salt and pepper. Keeps for several weeks and makes 1 ½ cups.

Honey Nut Filling

½ cup honey
½ cup chopped nuts

Combine and mix thoroughly the honey and nuts. Serve on buttered wheat toast. This makes one cup and will keep indefinitely.

Liederkranz and Onion Filling

3 oz. Liederkranz
2 Tbs. beer
2 Tbs. chives or finely chopped onion

Mash the Liederkranz with a fork until it is smooth and soft. Add the beer and blend to a smooth paste. Fold in chopped onions or chives. Spread on rye bread or toast.

Jellied Meats, Poultry, and Seafood (Aspic)

Start with a consommé (either canned or home made). If it does not jell when chilled, dissolve 1 Tbs. unflavored gelatin in ¼ cup cold water and stir into 1½ cups of the consommé while heating it. When this is done, lightly brush a mold with oil and pour some of the consommé into the mold. Pour enough to cover the bottom. Put the mold and the rest of the consommé into the regrigerator to chill. When the consommé in the mold is jelled and the rest of it is almost jelled, fold the ingredients of your choice into the aspic and pour it into the mold. Chill. To remove from the mold, dip mold in hot water briefly and slide a spatula into the sides to loosen it. Turn upside down over a plate and shake gently. It may then be cubed or sliced to be served on a sandwich.

Seafoods, meats, poultry, fruits, vegetables, and eggs may all be used in aspic salads. It is a good idea, though, to consider what you will be placing in the salad and to use a broth that will highlight the flavor. For example, chicken broth is good not only with chicken but with eggs and certain vegetables, whereas beef broth might be overpowering. Vegetable stock may be jellied with gelatin and used separately or added to a meat or poultry stock. Cooked meat may be added either sliced thinly or cubed. Vegetables and hard-boiled eggs may be added sliced or cubed. Fish should be flaked or finely chopped. Combine the seafood, poultry, or meat with appropriate herbs, spices, and other seasonings. (See listings of specific salads for suggestions.)

Liver and Bacon Filling

8 slices crisp bacon
¼ lb. beef liver
1 Tbs. grated onion
1 Tbs. minced chives
1 tsp. Worcestershire sauce
salt and pepper

Broil the liver just enough to remove the rawness. Grind the bacon and liver and add the onion, chives, Worcestershire sauce, and salt and pepper to taste. Mix thoroughly and serve on rye or Boston brown bread. Makes one cup and will keep a week.

Liver and Egg Filling

½ lb. beef liver
2 hard-boiled eggs
1 Tbs. grated onion
1 Tbs. minced parsley
1 Tbs. minced green pepper

few drops Tabasco sauce
½ tsp. Worcestershire sauce
2 Tbs. mayonnaise
salt and pepper
butter

Brown the liver in butter for 3 minutes. Cut into small pieces and grind. Add to the liver the fat from the pan, then the onion, parsley, green pepper, Tabasco sauce, Worcestershire sauce, and salt and pepper to taste. Put the eggs through a food chopper also and add to the mixture. Stir in the mayonnaise and blend thoroughly. Keeps a week and makes two cups.

Liver and Olive Filling

1 lb. beef liver
1 cup ripe olives
mayonnaise
salt and pepper

Cook the liver for 5 minutes in boiling salted water. Drain and grind with the olives. Moisten with mayonnaise and season to taste with salt and pepper. Store in a jar in the refrigerator. Serve on toast or hot waffles. Makes two cups.

Lox and Cream Cheese Spread

finely chopped lox
6 oz. cream cheese
finely chopped chives
1 Tbs. warm water

Work equal parts chives and lox into the cream cheese. It will take some kneading to work it into the cream cheese, so add a little at a time with water to soften it as necessary. You might find it easier to work the lox and chives into the cream cheese with your hands instead of with a spoon or fork. Serve on bagels or toasted rye bread.

Midinette Filling

½ cup honey
½ cup peanut butter
3 oz. sieved cream cheese
¼ cup seedless ground raisins

¼ cup ground nuts
salt and pepper

Combine the above ingredients and season to taste with salt and pepper. Mix thoroughly. Stores well in a jar in the refrigerator for up to two weeks. Serve on toast. This recipe makes two cups.

Onion Salad

chopped onion
vinaigrette sauce
paprika

Cover the chopped onions with the vinaigrette sauce and let sit in the refrigerator for a few hours. Drain, leaving only a little of the vinaigrette sauce on the onions. Sprinkle with paprika.

Orange and Grapefruit Marmalade, Cottage Cheese Filling

½ cup orange marmalade
½ cup grapefruit marmalade
1 cup well-drained cottage cheese, sieved
1 Tbs. minced chives or parsley
salt and pepper

Combine and mix well the orange and grapefruit marmalades and cottage cheese. Season with salt and pepper and chives or parsley. Store in a jar in the refrigerator for one week. Makes two cups. Serve on toast spread with peanut butter.

Parmesan Cheese and Anchovy Filling

3 Tbs. grated Parmesan cheese
½ tsp. anchovy paste
cream or evaporated milk

Mix together the cheese and anchovy paste. Add enough cream or evaporated milk to make a spreadable paste. Beat well and spread on any kind of bread or toast.

Parmesan Cheese and Shrimp Filling

3 Tbs. grated Parmesan cheese
1 Tbs. ground or finely chopped shrimp
mayonnaise

To the Parmesan cheese add the shrimp and enough mayonnaise to make a paste of spreadable consistency.

Peach and Nut Filling

1 cup fresh or canned peaches
½ cup ground nuts

½ cup ground chicken
1 tsp. ground cinnamon
salt and pepper

Mash the peaches to a pulp and combine with the nuts, chicken, and cinnamon. Season to taste with salt and pepper. Keeps one week and makes two cups.

Peanut Butter and Apple Filling

10 Tbs. pared, cored, and finely chopped apples
1 tsp. lemon juice
4 tsp. softened peanut butter
mayonnaise

To the apple, quickly add the lemon juice and mix with the peanut butter and mayonnaise. Serve on wheat toast. Makes one cup.

Peanut Butter Fluff

¾ cup peanut butter
¼ cup lemon juice
2 Tbs. sugar
salt
evaporated milk

Mix together the peanut butter, lemon juice, and sugar. Salt to taste and add enough evaporated milk to make a spreading consistency. Whip until light and fluffy. Serve on raisin bread. This will keep for one week and makes 1½ cups.

Pimiento Cheese and Deviled Ham Filling

1 cup pimiento cheese
1 can deviled ham
1 Tbs. dry mustard
½ cup peanut butter

Combine the cheese, deviled ham, mustard, and peanut butter together and blend well. Spread between 2 slices of any kind of bread.

Pimiento Cheese and Watercress Filling

pimiento cheese
mustard butter
minced watercress

Combine equal parts of cheese, watercress, and mustard butter and spread between 2 slices of bread.

Potato Salad

6 to 8 medium-sized potatoes

½ cup finely chopped onion
½ cup finely chopped celery
mayonnaise
salt and pepper

Boil potatoes with salt until tender. Drain and run them under cold water until cool enough to handle. Peel them and cut into small cubes. Add the chopped vegetables and mix in the mayonnaise. Season with salt and pepper. Let stand in the refrigerator for a while before using. May be used as a filling on rye bread or with other ingredients.

Variations:

1. Egg Potato Salad: Mix in mashed hard-boiled eggs.
2. Add finely chopped green pepper.
3. Sprinkle with parsley and/or paprika
4. Potato Nut Salad: Add chopped nuts to salad before serving.

Potato Salad, Hot (German Potato Salad)

3 medium-sized potatoes
2 strips crisp, minced bacon
2 Tbs. chopped onion
2 Tbs. chopped celery
2 Tbs. water
¼ cup vinegar
pinch of sugar
salt and pepper
pinch of dry mustard

Boil the potatoes with the skins on until tender. Peel and slice. Sauté the onions and celery and then add the remaining ingredients except the potatoes. Bring to boiling point, remove from heat, and add the potatoes. Good hot or cold.

Prunes and Nut Filling

cooked prunes
1 Tbs. lemon juice
1 cup ground nuts
salt and pepper

Sieve enough prunes to obtain 1 cup of pulp. Add the lemon juice and nuts. Season to taste with salt and pepper. Store in a jar in the refrigerator: it will last up to three weeks. Makes two cups.

Roquefort Cheese Filling

½ cup Roquefort cheese
½ cup cream cheese
1 tsp. Worcestershire sauce
salt and pepper

Combine and mix to a paste the Roquefort cheese and cream cheese. Add Worcestershire sauce and season to taste with salt and pepper. Makes one cup and will keep two weeks in the refrigerator.

Roquefort and Camembert Cheese Filling

½ cup Camembert cheese
½ cup Roquefort cheese
½ cup ground walnuts
1 tsp. Worcestershire sauce
1 tsp. ketchup
salt and pepper
few grains curry powder

Cream together the Camembert and Roquefort cheeses with the ground nuts. Add the Worcestershire sauce and ketchup and season with salt, pepper, and curry powder. Blend thoroughly and refrigerate. It will keep for months. Serve on pumpernickel bread. This recipe makes 1½ cups.

Roquefort Cheese and Nut Filling

Roquefort cheese
¼ cup finely chopped nuts (not ground)
mayonnaise
few drops Tabasco sauce
1 tsp. Worcestershire sauce

Cream the Roquefort cheese, adding mayonnaise to make it easier to cream. Add the nuts and mix well. Season with Tabasco sauce and Worcestershire sauce. Serve on rye or Boston brown bread. Keeps two weeks and makes one cup.

Roquefort Cheese and Watercress Filling

1 cup creamed Roquefort cheese
¼ cup finely chopped watercress
1 tsp. Worcestershire sauce
salt
paprika

Combine and mix well the above ingredients. Season to taste with salt and paprika. Will keep well in a jar in the refrigerator for up to two weeks. Serve on rye or Boston brown bread. Makes one cup.

Roquefort Cheese and Worcestershire Sauce Filling

2 Tbs. creamed Roquefort cheese
Worcestershire sauce

Mix together the cheese and the Worcestershire sauce and spread on toast.

Schnitzelbank Cheese Pot Filling

3½ lb. Camembert cheese   1 cup finely chopped olives
2 lb. Liederkranz cheese   ½ cup pimiento

¼ lb. Roquefort cheese
½ lb. butter
2 Tbs. flour

salt and pepper
cayenne
1 pt. cream

Scrape clean and free from outer skins the Camembert and Liederkranz cheeses and combine, in a copper or enamel pot, with the Roquefort cheese, butter, flour, and cream. Boil this until it melts and becomes smooth. Strain through a cloth or sieve and then mix in the olives and pimientos. Season highly with salt, pepper, and cayenne. Pack into a crock jar and let cool. Serve spread between 2 slices of rye or pumpernickel bread. The longer this mixture is kept in the crock jar, the better it will be.

Seafood Salad (Lobster Salad/Crabmeat Salad/Shrimp Salad)

½ cup seafood of your choice (or combine any of the above)
mayonnaise
celery seed

Chop the seafood into large pieces and moisten with mayonnaise. Season with celery seed.

Spicy American Cheese Filling

2 cups grated American cheese
1 cup ground dried beef
2 cups canned tomatoes (juice and pulp forced through a fine sieve)
salt and pepper
½ tsp. dry mustard
2 Tbs. tapioca
½ tsp. Worcestershire sauce

Place the tomatoes, salted and peppered to taste, and the mustard in a double boiler and cook until the mixture boils violently. Add the tapioca and continue boiling, stirring constantly until the tapioca is done, about 5 minutes. Add the American cheese and stir until melted. Remove from the water and add the beef and Worcestershire sauce. Blend well and cool. It will thicken as it cools. Keeps well in the refrigerator for one month. Makes five cups.

Spicy Ham Filling

1 cup ground cooked ham
⅓ cup finely chopped pickles
⅓ cup ground ripe olives
1 Tbs. finely minced parsley
1 Tbs. finely minced onion

1 Tbs. finely minced red pimiento
2 tsp. brown sugar
½ tsp. dry mustard
salt and pepper
mayonnaise

Combine the above ingredients. Moisten with the mayonnaise and season to taste with salt and pepper. Mix well and store in a jar in the refrigerator. It will keep for two weeks. Makes two cups.

Spicy Sardine Filling

2 cans sardines	3 Tbs. minced green pepper
2 slices bread	½ clove garlic, pressed
¼ cup milk (hot)	1 Tbs. Worcestershire sauce
2 hard-boiled eggs, ground	1 tsp. curry powder
salt and pepper	¼ cup ripe olives, ground
2 or 3 Tbs. vinegar	few drops Tabasco sauce
1 tps. sugar	4 Tbs. butter
3 Tbs. minced parsley	ketchup

Drain the sardines and mash to make 1 cup of paste. Combine with the bread which has been soaked in milk. Add to this all the ingredients except the ketchup. Mash and beat, using the ketchup to ease mashing. Makes about three cups and will keep three to four weeks.

Variation:

1. Substitute salmon for the sardines.

Spicy Savory Filling

½ cup minced cooked bacon
½ cup peanut butter
2 tps. Worcestershire sauce
few grains curry powder
ketchup

Mix together the bacon, peanut butter, Worcestershire sauce, and curry powder. Moisten with ketchup. Makes one cup. Does not keep long.

Spicy Shrimp and Caper Mayonnaise Filling

2 cups fresh or canned shrimp, cooked
¾ cup finely chopped celery
⅓ cup chopped capers
¼ cup mayonnaise
1 tsp. curry powder
1 tsp. Worcestershire sauce

Mince the shrimp very fine and combine with the celery, capers, mayonnaise, curry powder, and Worcestershire sauce. Blend thoroughly. Store in the refrigerator; it will last for two to three weeks. Makes 3½ cups.

Texas Filling

2½ cups any kind of leftover meats
2 Tbs. grated onions
½ cup tomato juice
salt
a pinch of cayenne
1 tsp. chili powder

Put the meat through a food chopper and mix in the onions. To the tomato juice add the salt, cayenne, and chili powder. Combine the meat, onions, and tomato juice and cook until thoroughly blended and mixture reaches the boiling point. Stir constantly. Cool or serve hot. Keeps well for two or three weeks. Makes two cups.

Tomato Salad

one tomato, sliced
vinaigrette sauce
minced parsley or chives

Pour vinaigrette sauce over the tomato slices and sprinkle with parsley or chives.

Tongue and Ham Filling

1 cup cold cooked tongue, ground
1 cup cold cooked ham, ground
paprika
salt and pepper
1 tsp. prepared mustard

1 tsp. Worcestershire sauce
1 Tbs. grated onion
1 Tbs. minced parsley
ketchup or mayonnaise

Mix the above ingredients together thoroughly, using either ketchup, mayonnaise, or both to moisten the mixture. Makes two cups and lasts in the refrigerator for two weeks.

Tongue and Horseradish Filling

1 cup cooked tongue, ground
3 Tbs. drained horseradish
3 Tbs. chili sauce
2 Tbs. minced green pepper
2 Tbs. minced onions

½ cup chopped ripe olives
1 Tbs. Worcestershire sauce
salt and pepper
mayonnaise

Mix the above ingredients together, seasoning to taste with salt and pepper and moistening with mayonnaise. Keeps in the refrigerator for two weeks and makes two cups.

Tongue and Pork Filling

1 cup cold, cooked pork, ground
1 cup cold, cooked tongue, ground
3 Tbs. green pepper
3 Tbs. parsley

3 Tbs. grated onion
salt and pepper
1 tsp. Worcestershire sauce
ketchup or mayonnaise

Combine the above ingredients and season to taste with salt and pepper. Moisten with either ketchup or mayonnaise. Pack in a jar and store in the refrigerator. Will keep for two weeks. Serve on raisin bread. Makes two cups.

Tuna Salad

7-oz. can of tuna
2 Tbs. chopped onion
½ cup chopped celery
mayonnaise
salt and pepper

Drain and flake the tuna fish and combine in a bowl with the onion and celery. Add mayonnaise and salt and pepper to taste.

Variations:

1. Add 1 medium grated carrot.
2. Add 1 Tbs. chopped sweet gherkin pickle and ¼ cup chopped black olives.

Vegetable Salad

green beans
kidney beans
cauliflower
onions
chick peas
green pepper

pimiento
2½ cups chopped vegetables (any or all of the above)
¼ cup **vinaigrette sauce**
pinch of tumeric

Mix the above ingredients together and let sit in the refrigerator before using.

PART 3

Suggested Sandwich Combinations

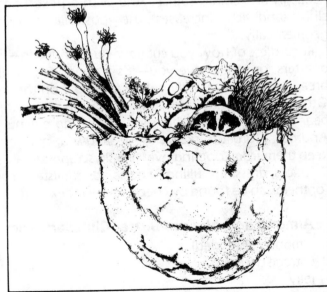

Club Sandwiches

Club sandwiches might be considered the casual epicure's answer to gluttony. They tend to be good-sized meals in themselves and are often pretty well balanced meals at that, satisfying all sorts of nutritional needs in one edible edifice. And with an extra tier to work with, the club sandwich increases the possibilities for creativity almost geometrically.

Regardless of how you cut your club sandwich—in half, diagonally in quarters, or what have you—it's a good idea to slice the top layer of bread or toast separately before putting it on the rest of the sandwich. Otherwise you may find yourself mashing everything together as you bear down with the knife, sending key ingredients off in all directions. And don't forget to skewer your sandwich quarters with toothpicks to keep them from toppling over like skyscrapers in an earthquake.

Sauces, dressings, fillings, and salads are listed in bold face; the recipes for them can be found by checking the index.

Almond and Almond Butter Club Sandwiches
almonds (shredded)
cottage cheese
jelly
peanut butter
lettuce

Bottom: Mix the almond, cottage cheese, and jelly. Spread on toast.
Top: Spread peanut butter on toast, then cover with lettuce

almond butter
lettuce
pineapple slice
mayonnaise

Bottom: Spread almond butter on bread, then cover with lettuce.
Top: Place the pineapple slice on bread, then cover with lettuce; spread mayonnaise on underside of the top piece of bread.

almond butter
marmalade
lettuce
sliced oranges

Bottom: Spread almond butter on toast, cover with marmalade, then with lettuce.
Top: Place orange slices on toast, then cover with lettuce.

almond butter
marshmallows (preferably miniature)
lettuce
fig date filling

Bottom: Spread almond butter on toast or bread. Heat the marshmallows until melted, then spread over the almond butter and cover with lettuce.
Top: Spread fig date filling on bread and cover with shredded lettuce.

Apple Club Sandwiches

apple
nuts
figs
lettuce
shredded pineapple
mayonnaise

Bottom: Spread mayonnaise on rye bread, then cover with sliced apple, chopped nuts, figs, and shredded lettuce.
Top: Spread mayonnaise on bread, then cover with shredded pineapple and shredded lettuce.

apple
peanut butter filling
lettuce
pineapple slice

Bottom: Spread peanut butter filling on toast, then cover with apple slices and shredded lettuce.
Top: Place pineapple slice on toast, then cover with shredded lettuce.

Apricot Club Sandwich

apricots, cooked, sieved
lettuce
cold cooked ham
mayonnaise

Bottom: Place apricots on toast, then cover with lettuce.
Top: Place ham on toast and cover with lettuce; spread mayonnaise on underside of top piece of toast.

Asparagus Tips Club Sandwich

asparagus tips
tomato
cole slaw
mayonnaise (optional)

Bottom: Place asparagus tips on whole wheat bread, then cover with tomato slices.
Top: Spread cole slaw (dressed with mayonnaise if desired) on bread.

Bacon Club Sandwiches

bacon
bean salad
tomato
lettuce

Bottom: Spread bean salad on bread, then cover with cooked bacon, and top with lettuce.
Top: Place tomato slices on bread, then cover with lettuce.

bacon
beef salad
watercress
lettuce

Bottom: Place cooked bacon on rye bread and cover with watercress.
Top: Spread beef salad on bread and cover with lettuce.

bacon
chicken (sliced)
anchovies
lettuce
tomato

Bottom: Place cooked bacon on toast, then cover with lettuce.
Top: Place sliced chicken on toast, then cover with anchovies, sliced tomatoes, and lettuce.

bacon
chicken (sliced)
lettuce
green pepper
tomato

Bottom: Place cooked bacon on toast, then cover with sliced chicken, and top with lettuce.
Top: Place green pepper slices on toast and cover with sliced tomatoes.

bacon
chicken livers
tomato
watercress

Bottom: Place cooked bacon on toasted rye and cover with broiled chicken livers.
Top: Place tomato slices on toast and cover with watercress.

bacon
cucumber
asparagus tips
lettuce
vinaigrette sauce

Bottom: Place cooked bacon on rye bread, cover with cucumber slices, and top with lettuce.
Top: Spread dressed shredded lettuce on bread and cover with asparagus tips dipped in vinaigrette sauce.

bacon
green pepper
cole slaw
tomato

Bottom: Place cooked bacon on toast and cover with green pepper slices.
Top: Spread cole slaw on toast, then cover with tomato slices.

Bacon
horseradish
banana
butter

lettuce leaves
peanut butter
mayonnaise

Bottom: Spread horseradish on toast, then cover with lettuce and cooked bacon.
Top: Spread peanut butter on toast, then cover with a sliced banana, and top with lettuce. Spread mayonnaise on underside of the top piece of toast.

bacon
lettuce leaves
orange marmalade
banana

Bottom: Place cooked bacon on rye bread, then cover with lettuce.
Top: Spread marmalade on bread, then cover with sliced banana and top with lettuce.

bacon
onion
tomato
watercress

Bottom: Place cooked bacon on rye bread, then cover with thinly sliced raw onion and top with lettuce.
Top: Place tomato slices on bread and cover with watercress.

bacon
potato salad
tomato
cole slaw

Bottom: Place cooked bacon on rye bread and cover with hot potato salad.
Top: Place tomato slices on bread and cover with cole slaw.

bacon
hot potato salad
egg salad
lettuce

Bottom: Place cooked bacon on bread, then cover with hot potato salad.
Top: Spread egg salad on bread and cover with lettuce.

bacon
potato salad
ham (sliced)
lettuce
mayonnaise

Bottom: Place cooked bacon on toast, cover with potato salad, then top with lettuce.
Top: Place thinly sliced ham on toast, then cover with lettuce. Spread mayonnaise on underside of top piece of toast.

bacon
Swiss cheese
lettuce or watercress
egg (hard-boiled)
anchovies

Bottom: Place cooked bacon on toast and cover with a thin slice of Swiss cheese, then top with lettuce or watercress.
Top: Place slices of hard-boiled egg and anchovies on toast, then cover with shredded lettuce.

    bacon
    Swiss cheese
    prepared mustard
    turkey (sliced)
    watercress
    mayonnaise

Bottom: Place cooked bacon on toasted rye bread. cover with thin slices of Swiss cheese, and spread mustard on cheese.
Top: Place sliced turkey on toast, then cover with watercress. Spread mayonnaise on underside of top piece of toast.

    bacon
    Swiss cheese
    tongue (sliced)
    tomato
    lettuce

Bottom: Place cooked bacon on bread and cover with thinly sliced Swiss cheese.
Top: Place sliced tongue on bread, cover with tomato, and top with lettuce.

    bacon
    tomato
    anchovy paste
    sardines
    lettuce

Bottom: Place cooked bacon on rye bread and cover with tomato slices.
Top: Spread anchovy paste on bread, cover with whole sardines, and top with lettuce.

    bacon
    tomato
    liverwurst
    cole slaw
    watercress

Bottom: Place cooked bacon on bread, cover with tomato slices, and top with watercress.
Top: Place thinly sliced liverwurst on bread and cover with cole slaw.

bacon
tomato
cole slaw
Swiss cheese
prepared mustard
lettuce

Bottom: Place cooked bacon on toast, cover with tomato slices, then with cole slaw.
Top: Place thinly sliced Swiss cheese on toast, cover with mustard, then top with lettuce.

bacon
tomato
vegetable salad
lettuce

Bottom: Place cooked bacon on whole wheat bread and cover with tomato slices.
Top: Spread vegetable salad on bread, then cover with lettuce.

bacon
tomato
onion
caviar
lettuce

Bottom: Place cooked bacon on toast and cover with tomato slices.
Top: Place thinly sliced raw onion on toast, cover with caviar, then top with lettuce.

bacon
watercress
salami
vegetable salad
lettuce

Bottom: Place cooked bacon on bread and cover with watercress.
Top: Place sliced salami on bread, cover with vegetable salad, and top with lettuce.

Beef Salad Club Sandwiches
beef salad
cole slaw
tomato
lettuce leaves

Bottom: Cover bread with lettuce leaves, beef salad, then cole slaw.
Top: Place tomato slices on bread and cover with lettuce.

beef salad
pickle relish
sliced cheese
lettuce leaves
watercress

Bottom: Cover bread with lettuce, beef salad, then with relish.
Top: Place cheese on bread and cover with watercress.

Caviar Club Sandwich
caviar
onion
tomato
watercress

Bottom: Spread caviar on toast, then cover with sliced onion.
Top: Place tomato slices on toast and cover with watercress.

Cheese Club Sandwiches
cheese (sliced)
grilled ham
lettuce
tomato
mayonnaise

Bottom: Spread mayonnaise on bread or toast. Cover with cheese and lettuce.
Top: Place ham on bread, cover with tomato slices, and top with lettuce.

cheese (sliced)
lettuce
mustard mayonnaise
peanut butter
jelly

Bottom: Spread mustard mayonnaise on bread, then cover with cheese and lettuce.
Top: Spread peanut butter on bread, then cover with lettuce; spread jelly on underside of top piece of bread.

Chicken Club Sandwiches

chicken (sliced)
asparagus tips
bacon
tomato
lettuce leaves

Bottom: Place sliced chicken on toast and cover with asparagus tips.
Top: Place broiled bacon on toast, then cover with tomato slices and lettuce.

chicken (sliced)
bacon
tomato
nuts (any kind)
lettuce leaves

Bottom: Place sliced chicken on rye bread, then cover with cooked bacon.
Top: Place tomato slices on bread, then cover with chopped nuts and top with lettuce.

Variation:

1. Substitute whole wheat bread for rye and cold sliced tongue for chopped nuts.

chicken (sliced)
bacon
lettuce leaves
green pepper
tomato

Bottom: Place sliced chicken on toast, cover with bacon, and top with lettuce.
Top: Place green pepper slices on toast and cover with tomato slices.

chicken (sliced)
bacon
tomato
olives
lettuce leaves

Bottom: Place sliced chicken on bread and cover with cooked bacon.
Top: Place tomato slices on bread, cover with chopped olives, and top with lettuce.

chicken (sliced)
celery stalks (small)
bacon
lettuce leaves
tomato

Bottom: Place chicken slices on rye bread, cover with celery stalks, and top with lettuce.
Top: Place bacon on bread and cover with tomato slices.

    chicken (sliced)
    green pepper
    bacon
    tomato
    2 anchovies
    lettuce leaves

Bottom: Place sliced chicken on rye bread, then cover with chopped green pepper and cooked bacon.
Top: Place tomato slices on bread, cover with anchovies, and top with lettuce.

    chicken (sliced)
    lettuce leaves
    shredded pineapple
    shredded red cabbage

Bottom: Place sliced chicken on toast and cover with lettuce.
Top: Spread shredded pineapple on toast, cover with shredded cabbage, then top with lettuce.

    chicken (sliced)
    shredded lettuce
    egg (hard-boiled)
    mayonnaise

Bottom: Place sliced chicken on bread, then cover with shredded lettuce mixed with mayonnaise.
Top: Place the egg on bread and cover with lettuce.

    chicken (sliced)
    lettuce leaves
    jelly (any kind)
    watercress

Bottom: Place sliced chicken on raisin bread and cover with lettuce.
Top: Spread jelly on bread and cover with chopped watercress.

    chicken (sliced)
    nuts (any kind)
    mayonnaise
    jelly (any kind)
    shredded lettuce

Bottom: Place sliced chicken on pumpernickel bread, then cover with nuts mixed with a little mayonnaise.

Top: Spread jelly on bread and cover with shredded lettuce.

Chicken Liver Club Sandwiches
chicken livers
bacon
lettuce leaves
tomato

Bottom: Cover nut bread with sautéed chicken livers, then with cooked bacon, and top with lettuce.

Top: Cover bread with lettuce and top with tomato slices.

chicken livers
red cole slaw
tomato
mustard mayonnaise

Bottom: Place broiled chicken livers on raisin bread and cover with red cole slaw.

Top: Place tomato slices on bread and cover with chopped watercress mixed with mustard mayonnaise.

chicken livers
tomato
lettuce leaves
bacon
cucumber

Bottom: Spread broiled, mashed chicken livers on toast, cover with broiled tomato slices, then top with lettuce.

Top: Place lettuce leaves on toast, cover with cooked bacon, then with sliced cucumber, and top with lettuce.

Chicken Salad Club Sandwiches
chicken salad
bacon
tomato
relish
lettuce leaves

Bottom: Spread chicken salad on nut bread, then cover with cooked bacon.

Top: Place tomato slices on bread, cover with relish, then top with lettuce.

chicken salad
cole slaw
boiled ham (sliced)
tomato
lettuce leaves

Bottom: Spread chicken salad on toasted rye bread, and cover with cole slaw.

Top: Place thinly sliced ham on bread, cover with tomato slices, and top with lettuce.

chicken salad
cucumber
cream cheese
3 anchovies
lettuce leaves

Bottom: Spread chicken salad on pumpernickel bread, cover with sliced cucumber, then top with lettuce.

Top: Spread bread with cream cheese, cover with anchovies, then top with lettuce.

chicken salad
green pepper
Swiss cheese
tomato
lettuce leaves

Bottom: Spread chicken salad on toasted rye bread, then cover with chopped green pepper.

Top: Place thinly sliced Swiss cheese on toast, cover with tomato slices, then top with lettuce.

chicken salad
lettuce leaves
sliced ham
Swiss cheese

Bottom: Spread chicken salad on pumpernickel bread, then cover with lettuce.

Top: Cover bread with thin slice of ham, and then with thin slices of Swiss cheese.

chicken salad
shredded lettuce
cold cooked, sliced tongue
tomato

Bottom: Cover Boston brown bread with chicken salad, then with shredded lettuce.

Top: Cover bread with sliced tongue, then with tomato slices, and top with lettuce.

chicken salad
olives
lettuce leaves
cheese (sliced)
tomato

Bottom: Spread chicken salad on toast, cover with chopped, pitted olives, and top with lettuce.

Top: Place thin slices of cheese on bread, cover with tomato slices, and top with lettuce.

chicken salad
pimientos
watercress
cold roast beef (sliced)
pickles
lettuce leaves

Bottom: Spread chicken salad on toast, cover with chopped pimientos, and top with chopped watercress.

Top: Place roast beef on bread, cover with chopped pickles, and top with lettuce.

chicken salad
spiced beets
cold tongue
tomatoe
lettuce leaves

Bottom: Spread chicken salad on bread, cover with chopped beets, then top with lettuce.

Top: Place thin slices of tongue on bread, cover with thinly sliced tomatoes, and top with lettuce.

chicken salad
tomato
asparagus tips
shredded lettuce

Bottom: Spread chicken salad on bread, then cover with tomato slices.

Top: Place asparagus tips on bread and cover with shredded lettuce.

chicken salad
tomato
vegetable salad
shredded lettuce

Bottom: Spread chicken salad on toast, cover with tomato slices, then top with shredded lettuce.
Top: Spread vegetable salad on toast, and cover with lettuce.

chicken salad
tomato
anchovies
shredded lettuce

Bottom: Spread chicken salad on rye bread, then cover with tomato slices.
Top: Cover bread with anchovies (to taste!), then top with shredded lettuce.

Corned Beef Club Sandwiches

corned beef
apple, cooking
prepared mustard
cheese (sliced)
lettuce leaves

Bottom: Place thinly sliced cold, cooked corned beef on toasted raisin bread, cover with slices of cooking apples that are lightly spread with mustard, then top with lettuce.
Top: Place slices of cheese on toast, then cover with lettuce.

corned beef
cabbage relish
crushed pineapple
lettuce leaves

Bottom: Place thinly sliced cold, cooked corned beef on toast and cover with cabbage relish.
Top: Spread well-drained crushed pineapple on toast and cover with lettuce.

corned beef
cole slaw
tomato
lettuce leaves

Bottom: Place thinly sliced cold, cooked corned beef on bread and cover with seasoned cole slaw.
Top: Place tomato slices on bread, and cover with lettuce.

corned beef (lean)
dill pickles
shredded lettuce
pickled beets (well drained)

Bottom: Place thinly sliced cold, cooked corned beef on rye bread, cover with thin slices of dill pickles, then top with lettuce.
Top: Place sliced pickled beets on bread and top with seasoned, shredded lettuce.

corned beef
horseradish
tomato
mayonnaise
lettuce leaves or watercress

Bottom: Place thin slices of cold, cooked corned beef on bread and top with horseradish.
Top: Place tomato slices on bread, cover with mayonnaise, and top with lettuce or watercress.

corned beef   Swiss cheese
prepared mustard   watercress
onion   **mustard mayonnaise**
lettuce

Bottom: Place thinly sliced cold, cooked corned beef on toasted rye bread, spread lightly with mustard, cover with very thin onion slices, and top with lettuce.
Top: Place thinly sliced Swiss cheese on toast and cover with chopped watercress mixed with mustard mayonnaise.

corned beef
spinach, chopped (uncooked)
cream cheese
lettuce or cabbage

Bottom: Place thinly sliced, cold corned beef on whole wheat bread, then cover with chopped spinach.
Top: Spread cream cheese mixed with shredded lettuce or cabbage on bread.

Crabmeat Club Sandwiches
crabmeat
apple
mayonnaise
onion
pineapple slice
lettuce leaves

Bottom: Spread crabmeat on toasted raisin bread, cover with cubed apple mixed with mayonnaise, and top with thinly sliced onion.
Top: Place pineapple slice on toast and cover with lettuce.

crabmeat
curried mayonnaise
red cabbage
sardines
lettuce leaves

Bottom: Spread crabmeat mixed with curried mayonnaise on toasted rye bread, then cover with shredded red cabbage.
Top: Cover toast with sardines and top with lettuce.

crabmeat	banana
ham (chopped)	lemon juice
mayonnaise	spinach (uncooked)
shredded lettuce	**vinaigrette sauce**

Bottom: Spread crabmeat mixed with ham (in equal parts) dressed with mayonnaise on bread, then top with shredded lettuce.
Top: Cover bread with sliced banana (sprinkled with lemon juice), then top with shredded spinach dressed with vinaigrette sauce.

crabmeat
lettuce leaves
peanut butter
cucumber
watercress

Bottom: Spread crabmeat mixed with mayonnaise on toast, and cover with lettuce.
Top: Spread peanut butter on toast, cover with thin slices of cucumber, and top with watercress.

crabmeat
mayonnaise
olives
lettuce leaves
cooked salmon
horseradish

Bottom: Spread crabmeat mixed with mayonnaise on bread, cover with olive slices, then top with lettuce.
Top: Cover bread with salmon, spread lightly with horseradish, then top with lettuce.

crabmeat
mayonnaise
raw red or white cabbage (shredded)
baked beans (cold)
lettuce leaves

Bottom: Spread crabmeat mixed with mayonnaise on whole wheat bread and cover with shredded cabbage.
Top: Spread baked beans on bread and cover with lettuce.

crabmeat
mayonnaise
onion
lettuce leaves
green bean salad

Bottom: Spread crabmeat mixed with mayonnaise on toast, cover with thinly sliced onion, and top with lettuce.
Top: Spread green bean salad on toast, then top with lettuce.

crabmeat
mayonnaise
cucumber
tomato
lettuce leaves
ketchup or tomato paste (optional)

Bottom: Spread crabmeat mixed with mayonnaise (to which ketchup or tomato paste may be added if desired) on toasted rye bread, cover with cucumber slices, then top with lettuce.
Top: Place tomato slices on toast and cover with lettuce.

crabmeat
mayonnaise
tomato
capers (optional)

prepared mustard (optional)
lettuce
dill pickle

Bottom: Spread crabmeat mixed with mayonnaise (to which may be added capers and mustard) on raisin bread, cover with tomato slices, then top with lettuce leaves
Top: Place dill pickles (sliced lengthwise) on bread and cover with shredded lettuce.

crabmeat
mayonnaise
tomato
egg salad
watercress

Bottom: Spread crabmeat mixed with mayonnaise on toast and cover with tomato slices.
Top: Spread egg salad on toast and top with watercress.

crabmeat
chopped nuts
mayonnaise
lettuce leaves
cold tongue

Bottom: Spread crabmeat mixed with chopped nuts and mayonnaise on toast, then cover with lettuce.

Top: Place thinly sliced cold tongue on toast, and top with lettuce.

ketchup (optional)	crabmeat
tomato	olives (black)
prepared mustard	lettuce

Bottom: Spread cleaned crabmeat on nut bread, cover with light spread of ketchup if desired, then with pitted chopped olives, and top with lettuce.

Top: Place tomato slices on bread, spread lightly with mustard, then top with shredded lettuce.

crabmeat
spinach (uncooked)
mayonnaise
egg salad
lettuce leaves

Bottom: Spread crabmeat mixed with mayonnaise on bread and cover with chopped spinach.

Top: Spread egg salad on bread and top with lettuce.

Date Club Sandwiches

mayonnaise	dates
lettuce leaves	cherries
toasted marshmallow	pineapple
shredded coconut	chopped nuts (any kind)

Bottom: Mix dates, pitted cherries, pineapple, nuts, and mayonnaise into a salad, spread on toasted rye bread, then cover with lettuce.

Top: Spread toasted marshmallow on toast, sprinkle with shredded coconut, then top with lettuce.

lettuce leaves	dates
prepared mustard	chopped nuts (any kind)
boiled ham (sliced)	mayonnaise
watercress	

Bottom: Cover toast with chopped dates and nuts mixed with mayonnaise and top with lettuce.

Top: Spread mustard on toast, cover with thin slice of cold boiled ham, then top with shredded watercress.

dates	lettuce leaves
peanuts	pineapple
cooking apple (cubed)	watercress
mayonnaise	

Bottom: Mix chopped dates, chopped peanuts, cubed apple, and mayonnaise, spread on bread, then top with lettuce.

Top: Place pineapple slice on bread, then top with several sprigs of watercress.

Deviled Egg Club Sandwiches
deviled egg
chicken salad
Spanish onion
watercress

Bottom: Cover toast with deviled egg, then with chicken salad, and top with lettuce.

Top: Cover toast with thinly sliced Spanish onion and top with watercress.

deviled egg
crabmeat salad
green onion or scallions
lettuce leaves

Bottom: Cover toast with deviled egg, then with crabmeat salad.

Top: Cover toast with either green onion (sliced thin) or scallions, then top with lettuce.

deviled egg
salmon salad
shredded lettuce
green pepper

Bottom: Cover toast with deviled egg, then with salmon salad, and top with lettuce.

Top: Place green pepper rings on toast, then cover with shredded lettuce.

deviled egg
sardine salad
tomato
lettuce

Bottom: Cover Boston brown bread with deviled egg, then with sardine salad.

Top: Place tomato slices on bread and cover with lettuce.

deviled egg
sardine salad
lettuce leaves
bacon
tomato
watercress

Bottom: Cover pumpernickel bread with deviled egg, then with sardine salad, and top with lettuce.
Top: Place cooked bacon on bread, cover with tomato slices, then top with watercress.

deviled egg
shrimp salad
cold tongue (sliced)
watercress

Bottom: Cover toast with deviled egg, then with shrimp salad.
Top: Place thinly sliced tongue on toast and top with seasoned watercress.

Egg Club Sandwiches
egg (hard-boiled)
anchovies
lettuce leaves
cold cooked tongue (sliced)
mayonnaise
watercress

Bottom: Cover rye bread with sliced egg, then with anchovies, and top with lettuce.
Top: Cover bread with thinly sliced tongue, spread lightly with mayonnaise, and top with watercress.

egg (hard-boiled)
anchovies
lettuce leaves
tomato

Bottom: Cover pumpernickel bread with sliced egg, then with anchovies, and top with lettuce.
Top: Cover bread with tomato slices and top with lettuce.

egg (hard-boiled)
bacon

lettuce leaves
lobster salad

Bottom: Cover rye bread with sliced egg, then with cooked bacon, and top with lettuce.
Top: Spread lobster salad on bread, then top with lettuce.

egg (hard-boiled)
bacon
olives
potato nut salad
lettuce leaves

Bottom: Cover bread with sliced egg, then with cooked bacon, and top with chopped olives.
Top: Spread potato nut salad on bread and top with lettuce.

egg (hard-boiled)
bacon
lettuce
baked beans (hot or cold)

Bottom: Cover toast with sliced egg, then with bacon, and top with shredded lettuce.
Top: Spread baked beans on toast and top with lettuce leaves.

egg (hard-boiled)
bacon
lettuce leaves
prepared mustard
watercress

Bottom: Cover toast with sliced egg, then with cooked bacon, and top with lettuce.
Top: Place tomato slices on toast, spread lightly with mustard, and top with watercress.

egg (hard-boiled)
celery
olives
lettuce leaves
sardines

Bottom: Cover bread with sliced hard-boiled egg, then with chopped celery mixed with chopped olives, and top with lettuce.
Top: Cover bread with sardines and top with lettuce.

egg (hard-boiled)
chicken liver (broiled or sautéed)

lettuce leaves
cheese (sliced)
prepared mustard
watercress

Bottom: Cover toast with sliced egg, then with chicken liver, and top with lettuce.

Top: Cover toast with cheese, spread lightly with mustard, and top with watercress.

egg (hard-boiled)
cole slaw
tomato
green pepper rings
lettuce leaves

Bottom: Cover toasted rye bread with sliced egg, then top with cole slaw.

Top: Cover toast with tomato slices, then with green pepper rings, and top with lettuce.

egg (hard-boiled)   cheese (sliced)
cucumber   prepared mustard
watercress   lettuce leaves
banana

Bottom: Cover date bread with sliced egg, then with sliced cucumber, and top with dressed shredded watercress.

Top: Place banana (sliced lengthwise) on bread, cover with cheese, spread with mustard, and top with lettuce.

egg (hard-boiled)
ham (minced)
lettuce leaves
cole slaw
watercress
chopped nuts

Bottom: Cover toast with sliced egg, then with minced ham, and top with lettuce.

Top: Spread cole slaw mixed with any kind of chopped nuts on toast and top with watercress.

egg (hard-boiled)
ham (sliced)
lettuce leaves
green bean salad

Bottom: Cover toast with sliced egg, then with thin slice of ham, and top with lettuce.

Top: Spread green bean salad on toast and top with lettuce.

egg (hard-boiled)
lettuce (shredded)
tomato
watercress

Bottom: Cover raisin bread with sliced hard-boiled egg, then with shredded lettuce.
Top: Cover bread with tomato slices and top with watercress.

egg (hard-boiled)
pimiento
cold ham (sliced)
relish
lettuce leaves

Bottom: Cover rye bread with sliced egg, then with pimiento ring.
Top: Cover bread with thinly sliced ham, spread with relish, then top with lettuce.

egg (hard-boiled)
red cole slaw
potato salad
lettuce leaves

Bottom: Cover rye bread with sliced egg and top with red cole slaw.
Top: Spread potato salad on bread, then top with lettuce.

egg (hard-boiled)
shrimp salad
lettuce
cold chicken (sliced)
mayonnaise

Bottom: Cover bread with sliced egg, then with shrimp salad, and top with lettuce leaves.
Top: Cover bread with sliced chicken, spread with mayonnaise, and top with shredded lettuce.

egg (hard-boiled)
Swiss cheese
prepared mustard
lettuce leaves
cold cooked ham (sliced)
tomato

Bottom: Cover toasted rye bread with sliced egg, then with Swiss cheese spread with mustard, and top with lettuce.

Top: Cover toast with thinly sliced cold ham, then with tomato slices, and top with lettuce.

egg (hard-boiled)
tomato
lettuce
tuna salad

Bottom: Cover Boston brown bread with thinly sliced egg, then with tomato slices, and top with lettuce leaves.
Top: Spread tuna salad on bread, then top with shredded lettuce.

egg (hard-boiled)
tomato
watercress
chicken salad
lettuce leaves

Bottom: Cover bread with sliced egg, then with tomato slices, and top with watercress.
Top: Spread chicken salad on bread and top with lettuce.

egg (hard-boiled)
tomato
cole slaw
ham salad
lettuce leaves

Bottom: Cover rye bread with sliced egg, then with tomato slices, and top with cole slaw.
Top: Spread ham salad on bread and cover with lettuce.

Egg Salad Club Sandwiches
egg salad
anchovies
vegetable salad
lettuce leaves

Bottom: Spread egg salad on rye bread, then cover with anchovies.
Top: Spread vegetable salad on bread and top with lettuce.

egg salad
anchovies
lettuce leaves
knockwurst
prepared mustard
cole slaw

Bottom: Spread egg salad on rye or pumpernickel bread, cover with anchovies, then top with lettuce.
Top: Cover bread with thinly sliced knockwurst, spread lightly with mustard, cover with cole slaw, and top with lettuce.

egg salad
anchovies
lettuce leaves
tomato

Bottom: Spread egg salad on toast, cover with anchovies, then top with lettuce.
Top: Cover toast with tomato slices, and top with lettuce.

egg salad
asparagus tips
cold sliced ham
cheese (sliced)
shredded lettuce

Bottom: Spread egg salad on whole wheat bread, then cover with asparagus tips.
Top: Place thin slice of ham on bread, cover with thin slice of cheese, then top with shredded lettuce.

egg salad
bacon
watercress
tomato
anchovies
lettuce leaves

Bottom: Spread egg salad on toasted whole wheat bread, cover with cooked bacon, then top with shredded watercress.
Top: Place tomato slices on toast, cover with anchovies, then top with lettuce.

egg salad
bacon
lettuce leaves
tomato
prepared mustard
green pepper

Bottom: Spread egg salad on toast, cover with cooked bacon, then top with lettuce.
Top: Place tomato slices on toast, spread with mustard, cover with green pepper rings, then top with lettuce.

egg salad
bacon
lettuce leaves
tomato
anchovies

Bottom: Spread egg salad on Boston brown bread, cover with cooked bacon, then top with lettuce.

Top: Cover bread with tomato slices, then with anchovies, and top with lettuce.

egg salad
bacon
lettuce leaves
Swiss cheese
prepared mustard
watercress

Bottom: Spread egg salad on bread, cover with cooked bacon, then top with lettuce.

Top: Cover bread with Swiss cheese, spread lightly with mustard, then top with watercress.

egg salad
bologna
watercress
tomato
prepared mustard

Bottom: Spread egg salad on rye bread, cover with thin slice of bologna, and top with shredded watercress.

Top: Cover bread with tomato slices, spread lightly with mustard, then top with lettuce.

egg salad
cole slaw
cold chicken (sliced)
lettuce leaves

Bottom: Spread egg salad on bread and cover with cole slaw.

Top: Place sliced chicken on bread and cover with lettuce.

egg salad
green pepper
lettuce
tuna salad

Bottom: Spread egg salad on rye bread, cover with green pepper rings, then top with shredded lettuce.

Top: Spread tuna salad on bread and top with lettuce leaves.

egg salad
green pepper
hot dogs
prepared mustard
lettuce leaves

Bottom: Spread egg salad on rye bread, then cover with green pepper rings.
Top: Place cooked hot dogs sliced lenghthwise on bread, spread lightly with mustard, then top with lettuce.

egg salad
green pepper
sardines
chopped nuts (any kind)
mayonnaise
lettuce leaves

Bottom: Spread egg salad on whole wheat bread and cover with green pepper rings.
Top: Cover bread with whole sardines (split in two), then with chopped nuts mixed with mayonnaise, and top with lettuce.

egg salad
pimientos
lettuce leaves
cold chicken (sliced)
bacon

Bottom: Spread egg salad on toast, cover with chopped pimientoes, then top with lettuce.
Top: Place chicken slices on toast, cover with cooked bacon, and top with lettuce.

egg salad
red cole slaw
cold tongue (sliced)
lettuce leaves

Bottom: Spread egg salad on raisin bread, then cover with red cole slaw.
Top: Cover bread with sliced tongue, then with tomato slices, and top with lettuce.

egg salad
roast beef cold, (sliced)
lettuce leaves
tomato
anchovies

Bottom: Spread egg salad on bread, cover with roast beef, and top with lettuce.
Top: Place tomato slices on bread, cover with anchovies, then top with lettuce.

egg salad
sardines
watercress
tomato
prepared mustard
lettuce leaves

Bottom: Spread egg salad on toast, cover with mashed sardines, then top with watercress.
Top: Place tomato slices on toast, spread with mustard, then top with lettuce.

egg salad
tomato
salmon
vinaigrette sauce
olives
lettuce leaves

Bottom: Spread egg salad on toasted rye bread and cover with tomato slices.
Top: Cover toast with flaked salmon mixed with vinaigrette sauce and chopped olives, then cover with lettuce.

egg salad
tomato
lettuce leaves
Spanish onion
caviar

Bottom: Spread egg salad on toast, cover with tomato slices, then top with lettuce.
Top: Cover toast with sliced Spanish onions, then with caviar, and top with lettuce.

egg salad
tomato
green bean salad
tomato
lettuce leaves

Bottom: Spread egg salad on rye bread, cover with tomato slices, then top with lettuce.
Top: Spread green bean salad on bread and top with lettuce.

egg salad
tomato
lettuce
sliced pineapple

Bottom: Spread egg salad on toasted raisin bread, cover with tomato slices, then top with lettuce leaves.
Top: Place pineapple slice(s) on toast and top with shredded lettuce.

egg salad
tomato
lettuce leaves
asparagus tips
ketchup (optional)

Bottom: Spread egg salad on bread, cover with tomato slices, then top with lettuce.
Top: Cover bread with asparagus tips dipped in ketchup (optional) and top with lettuce.

egg salad
tongue, cold (sliced)
cheese (sliced)
prepared mustard
lettuce leaves

Bottom: Spread egg salad on rye bread and cover with thinly sliced tongue.
Top: Cover bread with cheese, spread with mustard, then top with lettuce.

egg salad
watercress
tomato
cream cheese
walnuts (chopped)
lettuce leaves

Bottom: Spread egg salad on bread and cover with watercress.
Top: Place tomato slices on bread, cover with cream cheese mixed with chopped walnuts, then top with lettuce.

egg salad
watercress
pickle relish
asparagus tips
lettuce leaves

Bottom: Spread egg salad on rye bread and cover with watercress.
Top: Spread pickle relish on bread, cover with asparagus tips, then cover with lettuce.

egg salad
watercress
anchovies
bacon
lettuce leaves

Bottom: Spread egg salad on bread and top with chopped watercress.
Top: Cover bread with anchovies, then with cooked bacon, and top with lettuce.

Ham Club Sandwiches

cold ham (sliced)
cole slaw
tomato
prepared mustard
lettuce leaves

Bottom: Place thinly sliced ham on bread and cover with cole slaw.
Top: Cover bread with tomato slices, spread with mustard, and top with lettuce.

cold ham (sliced)
cream cheese
watercress
cold turkey (sliced)
cranberry sauce
lettuce leaves

Bottom: Place thinly sliced ham on toasted whole wheat bread, spread with cream cheese, and top with watercress.
Top: Place sliced turkey on toast, spread with cranberry sauce, and top with lettuce.

cold ham (sliced)
currant jelly
lettuce leaves
tomato
prepared mustard

Bottom: Place thinly sliced ham on orange date bread, spread with currant jelly, and top with lettuce.
Top: Cover bread with tomato slices, spread lightly with mustard, and top with lettuce.

cold ham (sliced)
dill pickles
lettuce leaves

tomato
horseradish

Bottom: Cover rye bread with thinly sliced ham, then with thinly sliced dill pickles, and top with lettuce.
Top: Cover bread with tomato slices, spread with horseradish, and top with lettuce.

cold ham (sliced)
horseradish
cheese (sliced)
tomato
lettuce leaves
watercress

Bottom: Place thinly sliced ham on toasted whole wheat bread, spread lightly with horseradish, cover with cheese, and top with lettuce.
Top: Cover toast with tomato slices, then top with watercress.

cold ham (sliced)
horseradish
lettuce leaves
green pepper

Bottom: Place thinly sliced ham on Boston brown bread, cover with horseradish, and top with lettuce.
Top: Cover bread with green pepper rings and top with lettuce.

cold ham (sliced)
horseradish
lettuce leaves
potato salad
watercress

Bottom: Place thinly sliced ham on rye bread, cover with horseradish, and top with lettuce.
Top: Spread potato salad on bread and top with watercress.

ham (sliced)   lettuce leaves
Jarlsberg cheese   mayonnaise
Muenster cheese   tomato
asparagus tips   French dressing (commercial)
crisp bacon

Bottom: Cover wheat toast with ham, then tomato slices, lettuce, and Muenster cheese. Top with mayonnaise.
Top: Place sautéed asparagus tips on toast, cover with bacon, Jarlsberg cheese, and lettuce dressed with French dressing.

cold ham (sliced)
Liederkranz cheese
lettuce leaves
tomato
horseradish

Bottom: Place thinly sliced ham on rye bread, cover with Liederkranz cheese, and top with lettuce.

Top: Cover bread with tomato slices, spread with horseradish, and top with lettuce.

cold ham (sliced)
prepared mustard
cheese (sliced)
lettuce leaves
tomato
anchovies

Bottom: Place thinly sliced ham on toasted rye bread, spread with mustard, cover with cheese, then top with lettuce.

Top: Cover toast with tomato slices, then with anchovies, and top with lettuce.

cold ham (sliced)
prepared mustard
tomato
lettuce leaves
green bean salad
mayonnaise (optional)

Bottom: Place thinly sliced ham on whole wheat bread, spread with mustard, cover with tomato slices, and top with lettuce.

Top: Spread green bean salad (mixed with mayonnaise if desired) on bread and top with lettuce.

cold ham (sliced)
prepared mustard
cold tongue
watercress
Swiss cheese
lettuce leaves

Bottom: Place thinly sliced ham on rye bread, spread lightly with mustard, and top with watercress.

Top: Place thinly sliced tongue on bread, cover with Swiss cheese, and top with lettuce.

cold ham (sliced)
mustard pickle
lettuce
potato nut salad
lettuce leaves

Bottom: Place thinly sliced ham on rye bread, cover with thinly sliced mustard pickle, and top with lettuce.
Top: Spread potato nut salad on bread, and top with lettuce.

cold ham (sliced)
pickle relish
lettuce leaves
asparagus tips

Bottom: Place thinly sliced ham on rye bread, cover with pickle relish, and top with lettuce.
Top: Cover bread with asparagus tips, and top with lettuce.

cold ham (sliced)
potato salad
lettuce leaves
tomato
prepared mustard

Bottom: Place thinly sliced ham on rye bread, cover with potato salad and top with lettuce.
Top: Place tomato slices on bread, spread with mustard, and top with lettuce.

cold ham (sliced)
Swiss cheese
lettuce leaves
bacon
tomato

Bottom: Place thinly sliced ham on toast, cover with Swiss cheese, and top with lettuce.
Top: Place cooked bacon on toast, cover with tomato slices, and top with lettuce.

cold ham (sliced)
Swiss cheese
lettuce leaves
tomato

Bottom: Place thinly sliced ham on bread, cover with Swiss cheese, and top with lettuce.
Top: Cover bread with tomato slices and top with lettuce.

cold ham (sliced}
tomato
celery leaves
peanut butter
pepper relish
lettuce leaves

Bottom: Place thinly sliced ham on toast, cover with tomato slices, and top with chopped celery leaves.
Top: Spread peanut butter on toast, cover with pepper relish, and top with lettuce.

cold ham (sliced)
tomato
cucumber salad
lettuce leaves
egg salad
liverwurst

Bottom: Place thinly sliced ham on toast, cover with tomato slices, then with cucumber salad, and top with lettuce.
Top: Spread egg salad on toast, cover with thinly sliced liverwurst, and top with lettuce.

cold ham (sliced)
tomato
lettuce leaves
Bermuda onion
celery salad

Bottom: Place thinly sliced ham on toasted rye bread, cover with tomato slices, and top with lettuce.
Top: Cover toast with thinly sliced Bermuda onion, then with celery salad, and top with lettuce.

cold ham (sliced)
watercress
potato salad
lettuce leaves

Bottom: Place thinly sliced ham on pumpernickel bread, then cover with chopped watercress.
Top: Spread potato salad on bread and cover with lettuce.

cold ham (sliced)
watercress
tomato
bacon
lettuce leaves

Bottom: Place thinly sliced ham on rye bread, and cover with dressed, chopped watercress.
Top: Cover bread with tomato slices, then with cooked bacon, and top with lettuce.

ham (minced)
prepared mustard
egg salad
lettuce leaves
tomato

Bottom: Cover bread with minced ham mixed with mustard, then with egg salad, and top with lettuce.
Top: Cover bread with tomato slices, then top with lettuce.

Ham Salad Club Sandwiches
ham salad
anchovies
lettuce
tomato
vinaigrette sauce

Bottom: Spread ham salad on rye bread, cover wtih anchovies, and top with lettuce leaves.
Top: Cover bread with tomato slices, then with shredded lettuce dressed with vinaigrette sauce.

ham salad
artichoke heart
lettuce leaves
tomato
anchovy paste

Bottom: Spread ham salad on rye bread, cover with sliced artichoke heart, and top with lettuce.
Top: Cover bread with tomato slices, spread with anchovy paste, and top with lettuce.

ham salad
asparagus tips
lettuce leaves
tomato
prepared mustard

Bottom: Spread ham salad on toast, cover with asparagus tips, and top with lettuce.

Top: Cover toast with tomato slices, spread lightly with mustard, and top with lettuce.

ham salad
corn
mayonnaise
watercress
chicken (sliced)
tomato
lettuce leaves

Bottom: Spread ham salad on toast, cover with corn, dressed with mayonnaise, and top with watercress.
Top: Cover toast with thinly sliced chicken, then with tomato slices, and top with lettuce.

ham salad
dill pickles
lettuce leaves
tomato
horseradish
cucumber

Bottom: Spread ham salad on rye bread, cover with thinly sliced dill pickles, and top with lettuce.
Top: Cover bread with tomato slices, spread lightly with horseradish, cover with thinly sliced cucumber, and top with lettuce.

ham salad
egg (hard-boiled)
lettuce leaves
caviar
onion

Bottom: Spread ham salad on toasted rye bread, cover with sliced egg, and top with lettuce.
Top: Spread caviar on toast, cover with minced onion, and top with lettuce.

ham salad
gherkin pickles
lettuce leaves
vegetable salad

Bottom: Spread ham salad on rye bread, cover with thinly sliced sweet-sour gherkin pickles, and top with lettuce.
Top: Spread bread with vegetable salad and top with lettuce.

ham salad
green pepper
watercress
potato salad
lettuce leaves

Bottom: Spread ham salad on rye bread, cover with green pepper rings, and top with watercress.
Top: Spread potato salad on bread and top with lettuce.

ham salad
lettuce leaves
tomato
watercress

Bottom: Spread ham salad on toast and top with lettuce.
Top: Cover toast with tomato slices, and top with watercress.

ham salad
shredded lettuce
green pepper
tomato
watercress

Bottom: Spread ham salad on toast and top with shredded lettuce mixed with chopped green pepper.
Top: Cover toast with broiled tomato slices and top with watercress.

ham salad
pickle relish
lettuce leaves
tomato
Swiss cheese (or American cheese)

Bottom: Spread ham salad on rye (or pumpernickel) bread, cover with pickle relish, and top with lettuce.
Top: Cover bread with tomato slices, then with thinly sliced Swiss or American cheese, and top with lettuce.

ham salad
pickle relish
lettuce leaves
bacon
tomato

Bottom: Spread ham salad on rye bread, cover with pickle relish, and top with lettuce.
Top: Place cooked bacon on bread, cover with tomato slices, and top with lettuce.

ham salad
pimiento
lettuce
navy bean salad

Bottom: Spread ham salad on bread, cover with red pimientos, and top with shredded lettuce.
Top: Spread navy bean salad on bread and top with lettuce leaves.

ham salad
pineapple
lettuce leaves
tomato
horseradish

Bottom: Spread ham salad on rye bread, cover with shredded pineapple, and top with lettuce.
Top: Cover bread with tomato slices, spread with horseradish, and top with lettuce.

ham salad
red cole slaw
tomato
horseradish
watercress

Bottom: Spread ham salad on rye bread, then cover with red cole slaw.
Top: Cover bread with tomato slices, then with horseradish, and top with watercress.

ham salad
spinach leaves, raw
lettuce leaves
Bermuda onion
egg salad

Bottom: Spread ham salad on bread, cover with chopped, raw spinach, and top with lettuce.
Top: Cover bread with thinly sliced onion, then with egg salad, and top with lettuce.

ham salad
Swiss cheese
prepared mustard
lettuce leaves
apple

Bottom: Spread ham salad on rye bread, cover with Swiss cheese, spread lightly with mustard, and top with lettuce.

Top: Cover bread with pared, cored apple slices, and top with lettuce.

ham salad
tomato
lettuce
Spanish onion
caviar

Bottom: Spread ham salad on whole wheat bread, cover with tomato slices, and top with shredded lettuce.
Top: Cover bread with thinly sliced onion, spread with caviar, and top with lettuce leaves.

ham salad
tomato
lettuce
potato salad

Bottom: Spread ham salad on whole wheat bread, cover with tomato slices, and top with lettuce leaves.
Top: Spread potato salad on bread and cover with shredded lettuce.

ham salad
watercress
tomato
anchovies
lettuce leaves

Bottom: Spread ham salad on rye bread and cover with watercress.
Top: Cover bread with tomato slices, then with anchovies, and top with lettuce.

Hamburger Club Sandwiches
hamburger
American cheese
lettuce leaves
bacon
prepared mustard

Bottom: Cover whole wheat bread with broiled hamburger, then with American cheese, and top with lettuce.
Top: Cover bread with broiled bacon, spread with prepared mustard, and top with lettuce.

hamburger
bacon
lettuce leaves

Swiss cheese
prepared mustard

Bottom: Cover toast with broiled hamburger, then with chopped bacon, and top with lettuce.

Top: Cover toast with thinly sliced Swiss cheese, spread with prepared mustard, and top with lettuce.

hamburger
bean salad
lettuce leaves
orange marmalade
nuts
watercress

Bottom: Cover orange date bread with broiled hamburger, then with bean salad, and top with lettuce.

Top: Spread bread with orange marmalade, mixed in equal parts with chopped nuts, and top with watercress.

hamburger
Bermuda onion
watercress
ham (sliced)
dill pickles
lettuce leaves

Bottom: Cover rye bread with broiled hamburger, then with thinly sliced Bermuda onion, and top with watercress.

Top: Cover bread with thinly sliced, cold, cooked ham, then with thinly sliced dill pickles, and top with lettuce.

hamburger
dill pickles
watercress
Bermuda onion
tomato
lettuce leaves

Bottom: Cover rye bread with broiled hamburger, then with thinly sliced dill pickles, and top with chopped watercress.

Top: Cover bread with thinly sliced Bermuda onion, then with tomato slices, and top with lettuce.

hamburger
egg (hard-boiled)
watercress
orange marmalade
shredded lettuce

Bottom: Cover nut bread with broiled hamburger, then with sliced, hard-boiled egg, and top with watercress.
Top: Spread orange marmalade on bread and top with shredded lettuce.

hamburger
ham (sliced)
prepared mustard
lettuce leaves
potato nut salad
lettuce leaves

Bottom: Cover rye bread with broiled hamburger, then with a thin slice of ham, spread with prepared mustard, and top with lettuce.
Top: Spread bread with potato nut salad and top with lettuce.

hamburger
horseradish
American cheese
prepared mustard
· lettuce leaves

Bottom: Cover toast with fried hamburger, then spread with prepared horseradish, and top with lettuce.
Top: Cover toast with thinly sliced American cheese, spread with prepared mustard, and top with lettuce.

hamburger
lettuce
chicken salad

Bottom: Cover white bread with broiled hamburger and top with shredded lettuce.
Top: Spread bread with chicken salad and top with lettuce leaves.

hamburger
Liederkranz cheese
lettuce leaves
tongue (sliced)
tomato

Bottom: Cover pumpernickel or rye bread with broiled hamburger, then with Liederkranz cheese, and top with lettuce.
Top: Cover bread with tongue slices, then with tomato slices, and top with lettuce.

hamburger
mustard pickles
watercress

pineapple
lettuce leaves

Bottom: Cover rye bread with hamburger, then with mustard pickles, and top with watercress.

Top:Cover bread with a slice of pineapple and top with lettuce.

hamburger
onions
lettuce leaves
American cheese
horseradish

Bottom: Cover Boston brown bread with broiled hamburger, then with cold sautéed onions, and top with lettuce.

Top: Cover bread with a thin slice of American cheese, spread with prepared horseradish, and top with lettuce.

hamburger
pickle relish
lettuce
cucumber salad

Bottom: Cover rye bread with broiled hamburger, then with pickle relish, and top with shredded lettuce.

Top: Spread bread with well-drained cucumber salad and top with lettuce leaves.

hamburger
pineapple
lettuce leaves
tomato
prepared mustard

Bottom: Cover raisin bread with broiled hamburger, then with well-drained, shredded pineapple, and top with lettuce.

Top: Cover bread with tomato slices, spread with prepared mustard, and top with lettuce.

hamburger
sauerkraut
tomato
bacon
lettuce leaves

Bottom: Cover pumpernickel or rye bread with broiled hamburger, then with well-drained sauerkraut.

Top: Cover bread with tomato slices, chopped bacon, and top with lettuce.

hamburger
tomato
watercress
curried egg
lettuce leaves

Bottom: Cover toast with broiled hamburger, then with tomato slices, and top with watercress.
Top: Cover toast with cold curried egg and top with lettuce.

hamburger
tomatoes
lettuce leaves
green bean salad

Bottom: Cover toast with broiled hamburger, then with hot fried tomatoes, and top with lettuce.
Top: Spread toast with green bean salad and top with lettuce.

hamburger
watercress
egg salad
lettuce leaves

Bottom: Cover toast with hamburger and top with chopped watercress.
Top: Spread egg salad on toast and top with lettuce.

hamburger
watercress
vinaigrette sauce
cream cheese
raspberry jam
lettuce leaves

Bottom: Cover raisin bread with broiled hamburger, then with chopped watercress dressed with vinaigrette sauce.
Top: Spread bread with cream cheese, mixed in equal parts with raspberry jam, and top with lettuce.

Herring Club Sandwiches
herring filets
Bermuda onion
lettuce leaves
tomato
prepared mustard
watercress

Bottom: Cover rye bread with well-drained herring filets, then with thinly sliced Bermuda onions, and top with lettuce.
Top: Cover bread with tomato slices, spread with prepared mustard, and top with watercress.

herring filets
cucumber salad
lettuce leaves
American cheese
watercress

Bottom: Cover whole wheat bread with well-drained herring filets, spread with cucumber salad, and top with lettuce.
Top: Cover bread with American cheese and top with watercress.

herring filets
dill pickles
lettuce leaves
tuna salad

Bottom: Cover rye bread with well-drained herring filets, then with thinly sliced dill pickles, and top with lettuce.
Top: Spread bread with tuna salad and top with lettuce.

herring filets
green bean salad
lettuce leaves
tomato
watercress

Bottom: Cover toasted rye bread with well-drained herring filets, then spread with well-drained green bean salad, and top with lettuce.
Top: Cover toast with tomato slices and top with watercress.

herring filets
potato salad
lettuce leaves
tomato
prepared mustard
horseradish

Bottom: Cover toasted pumpernickel bread with well-drained herring filets, then spread with potato salad, and top with lettuce.
Top: Cover toast with tomato slices, spread with prepared mustard and horseradish, mixed in equal parts, and top with lettuce.

herring filets
red cole slaw
Bermuda onion
pimiento
lettuce leaves

Bottom: Cover rye bread with well-drained herring filets, then with red cole slaw, and top with lettuce.
Top: Cover bread with thinly sliced Bermuda onion, then with pimiento slice, and top with lettuce.

herring salad
Swiss cheese
prepared mustard
lettuce leaves

Bottom: Spread rye bread with herring salad.
Top: Cover bread with thinly sliced Swiss cheese, spread lightly with prepared mustard, and top with lettuce.

herring fillets
tomato
anchovy paste
lettuce
green pepper
dill pickles
watercress

Bottom: Cover rye bread with well-drained herring filets, then with tomato slices spread lightly with anchovy paste, and top with lettuce.
Top: Cover bread with green pepper rings, then with thinly sliced dill pickles, and top with watercress.

herring filets
tomato
lettuce leaves
crabmeat salad

Bottom: Cover pumpernickel bread with well-drained herring filets, then with tomato slices, and top with lettuce.
Top: Spread bread with crabmeat salad and top with lettuce.

herring filets
tomato
lettuce leaves
salmon salad

Bottom: Cover toasted rye bread with well-drained herring filets, then with tomato slices, and top with lettuce.

Top: Spread toast with salmon salad and top with lettuce.

Honey Club Sandwiches
honey
almond paste
lettuce leaves
cream cheese

Bottom: Spread honey on orange bread, then spread with almond paste, and top with lettuce.
Top: Spread bread with cream cheese and top with lettuce.

honey
banana
shredded lettuce
cream cheese
currant jelly

Bottom: Spread honey on raisin bread, then cover with sliced banana, and top with shredded lettuce.
Top: Spread bread with cream cheese and currant jelly mixed in equal parts and top with shredded lettuce.

honey
ham (sliced)
watercress
cranberry sauce
nuts
lettuce leaves

Bottom: Spread nut bread with honey, then cover with sliced ham, and top with watercress.
Top: Spread bread with cranberry sauce and nuts mixed in equal parts and top with lettuce.

honey
Liederkranz cheese
watercress
tomato
shredded lettuce

Bottom: Spread honey on rye bread, then cover with Liederkranz cheese, and top with chopped watercress.
Top: Cover the bread with tomato slices and top with shredded lettuce.

honey
pineapple
lettuce
persimmon
lemon juice

Bottom: Spread honey on orange biscuit, then sprinkle generously with well-drained, shredded pinapple, and top with lettuce leaves

Top: Cover the biscuit with the pulp of ripe persimmon, mixed with a few drops of lemon juice, and top with shredded lettuce.

honey
raisins
lettuce leaves
cream cheese
nuts (any kind)

Bottom: Spread honey on raisin bread, then sprinkle generously with puffed (parboiled) seedless raisins, and top with lettuce.

Top: Spread bread with cream cheese, then sprinkle generously with chopped nuts, and top with lettuce.

honey
turkey (sliced)
lettuce leaves
cream cheese
olives
nuts

Bottom: Spread honey on Boston brown bread, then cover with thinly sliced cold turkey, and top with lettuce.

Top: Spread bread with mixture of cream cheese, chopped olives, and nuts, mixed in equal parts, and top with lettuce.

honey
walnuts
lettuce leaves
marshmallows
coconut

Bottom: Spread honey on orange bread, then sprinkle generously with chopped walnuts, and top with lettuce.

Top: Cover bread with toasted marshmallows, then with shredded coconut.

Jellied Meat Club Sandwiches

jellied chicken
lettuce leaves
tomato
horseradish
prepared mustard

Bottom: Cover white bread with jellied chicken and top with lettuce.
Top: Cover bread with tomato slices, then spread with horseradish and prepared mustard mixed in equal parts, and top with lettuce.

jellied crabmeat
lettuce leaves
green bean salad

Bottom: Cover white bread with jellied crabmeat and top with lettuce.
Top: Spread bread with green bean salad and top with lettuce.

jellied minced ham
cooking apples
lettuce leaves
cucumber
cole slaw

Bottom: Cover toasted rye bread with jellied minced ham, then with a pared, cored cooking apple, and top with lettuce.
Top: Cover toast with sliced cucumber, then with cole slaw, and top with lettuce.

jellied lobster
watercress
tomato
prepared mustard

Bottom: Cover toast with jellied lobster and top with watercress.
Top: Cover toast with tomato slices, then spread with prepared mustard, and top with watercress.

jellied ox tongue
watercress
Swiss cheese
prepared mustard
lettuce leaves

Bottom: Cover whole wheat bread with jellied ox tongue and top with watercress.
Top: Cover bread with Swiss cheese, then spread with prepared mustard, and top with lettuce.

jellied turkey
watercress
bacon
tomato
prepared mustard
lettuce leaves

Bottom: Cover white bread with jellied turkey and top with watercress.
Top: Cover bread with broiled bacon, then with tomato slices spread with prepared mustard, and top with lettuce.

jellied veal
watercress
tomato
horseradish
lettuce leaves

Bottom: Cover white bread with jellied veal and top with watercress.
Top: Cover bread with tomato slices spread with prepared horseradish, and top with lettuce.

Jelly Club Sandwich
jelly (any kind)
banana
watercress
peanut butter
shredded lettuce

Botom: Spread orange bread with jelly, then cover with sliced banana, and top with chopped watercress.
Top: Spread bread with peanut butter and top with dressed lettuce.

Liverwurst Club Sandwiches
liverwurst
bacon
lettuce leaves
anchovy filets
tomato

Bottom: Cover toasted whole wheat bread with sliced liverwurst, then with broiled bacon, and top with lettuce.
Top: Cover toast with anchovy filets, then with tomato slices, and top with lettuce.

liverwurst
cole slaw
lettuce leaves

American cheese
prepared mustard

Bottom: Cover toasted rye bread with sliced liverwurst, then with cole slaw, and top with lettuce.
Top: Cover toast with American cheese, spread with prepared mustard, and top with lettuce.

liverwurst
egg (hard-boiled)
lettuce leaves
tomato
onion
prepared mustard

Bottom: Cover rye bread with liverwurst, then with sliced hard-boiled egg, and top with lettuce.
Top: Cover rye bread with tomato slices, then with grated onion mixed with prepared mustard, and top with lettuce.

liverwurst
assorted fruits
nuts (any kind)
lettuce leaves
ham (sliced)
tomato

Bottom: Cover rye bread with liverwurst, then with well-drained, chopped, assorted fruits, and top with lettuce.
Top: Cover bread with thinly sliced cold ham, then with tomato slices, and top with lettuce.

liverwurst
horseradish
cucumber
tongue (sliced)
prepared mustard
lettuce leaves

Bottom: Cover rye bread with liverwurst, spread with horseradish, and top with sliced, pared cucumber.
Top: Cover bread with sliced tongue, spread with prepared mustard, and top with lettuce.

liverwurst
prepared mustard
Bermuda onion
lettuce

corned beef
horseradish

Bottom: Cover toasted roll with liverwurst spread with prepared mustard, then with thinly sliced Bermuda onion, and top with shredded lettuce.

Top: Cover roll with corned beef, spread with horseradish and mustard mixed in equal parts, and top with lettuce leaves.

liverwurst
pickle relish
lettuce leaves
bacon
tomato

Bottom: Cover toasted rye bread with sliced liverwurst, spread with pickle relish, and top with lettuce.

Top: Cover toast with broiled bacon, then with tomato slices, and top with lettuce.

liverwurst
potato salad
lettuce leaves
Swiss cheese
mustard

Bottom: Cover rye bread with liverwurst, then with potato salad, and top with lettuce.

Top: Cover bread with Swiss cheese, spread with prepared mustard, and top with lettuce.

liverwurst
red cole slaw
lettuce leaves
Roquefort cheese

Bottom: Cover whole wheat bread with liverwurst, then with red cole slaw, and top with lettuce.

Top: Cover bread with Roquefort cheese and top with lettuce.

liverwurst
tomato
prepared mustard
lettuce leaves
American cheese
horseradish

Bottom: Cover toasted rye bread with slices of liverwurst, then with tomato slices spread with prepared mustard, and top with lettuce.

Top: Cover toast with American cheese, spread with prepared horseradish and top with lettuce.

liverwurst
watercress
cream cheese
nuts (any kind)
lettuce leaves

Bottom: Cover toast with sliced liverwurst and top with chopped watercress.
Top: Spread toast with cream cheese and nuts mixed in equal parts and top with lettuce.

Lobster Club Sandwiches

lobster	nuts (any kind)
ketchup	olives
lettuce leaves	mayonnaise
tomato	

Bottom: Cover rye bread with coarsley chopped lobster, then spread with ketchup, and top with lettuce.
Top: Cover bread with tomato slices, spread with chopped nuts and olives mixed with mayonnaise, and top with lettuce.

lobster	tomato
mayonnaise	prepared mustard
watercress	green pepper rings
lettuce leaves	

Bottom: Cover whole wheat bread with chopped lobster, mixed with equal parts of mayonnaise and chopped watercress, and top with lettuce.
Top: Cover bread with tomato slices, spread with prepared mustard, then cover with green pepper rings, and top with lettuce.

lobster
tartar sauce
capers
lettuce
prepared mustard
sautéed mushrooms

Bottom: Cover white bread with coarsely chopped lobster mixed with tartar sauce and capers, and top with lettuce.
Top: Cover bread with sautéed mushrooms and top with lettuce.

lobster salad
nuts (any kind)
mayonnaise
lettuce leaves
pineapple

Bottom: Spread toast with lobster salad, nuts, and mayonnaise, mixed in equal parts, and top with lettuce.

Top: Cover toast with a slice of well-drained pineapple and top with lettuce.

Mushroom Club Sandwiches
broiled mushrooms
chicken (sliced)
watercress
bacon
tomato
lettuce leaves

Bottom: Cover toast with broiled, well-drained mushrooms, then with sliced chicken, and top with watercress

Top: Cover toast with broiled bacon, then with tomato slices, and top with lettuce.

sautéed mushrooms
bacon
lettuce leaves
tomato
horseradish

Bottom: Cover toast with sliced, sautéed mushrooms, chopped broiled bacon, and top with lettuce.

Top: Cover toast with tomato slices, spread with prepared horseradish, and top with lettuce.

sautéed mushrooms
crabmeat
watercress
tuna salad
lettuce leaves

Bottom: Cover toast with sautéed sliced mushrooms, mixed with flaked crabmeat, and top with watercress.

Top: Spread tuna salad on toast and top with lettuce.

sautéed mushrooms
egg (hard-boiled)
watercress

pineapple
lettuce

Bottom: Cover toasted raisin bread with sautéed sliced mushrooms, mixed with chopped hard-boiled egg, and top with chopped watercress.

Top: Cover toast with well-drained pineapple slice and top with lettuce.

sautéed mushrooms
onions
lettuce
tomato
bacon

Bottom: Cover toasted rye bread with sautéed sliced mushrooms, mixed with fried onions, and top with shredded lettuce.

Top: Cover toast with tomato slices, then with broiled bacon, and top with lettuce leaves.

Nut Club Sandwiches

nuts (any kind)
cranberry jelly
watercress
turkey (sliced)
horseradish
lettuce leaves

Bottom: Cover toasted French bread with chopped nuts and cranberry jelly, mixed in equal parts, and top with chopped watercress.

Top: Cover toast with sliced cold turkey, spread with prepared horseradish, and top with lettuce.

nuts (any kind)   veal (sliced)
dried figs   dill pickle
mayonnaise   lettuce leaves
watercress

Bottom: Cover orange peel bread with chopped nuts and chopped dried figs mixed with mayonnaise and top with watercress.

Top: Cover bread with sliced veal, then with thinly sliced dill pickle, and top with lettuce.

nuts (any kind)
chopped liver
watercress
apple celery salad
mayonnaise
lettuce leaves

Bottom: Cover rye bread with nuts mixed with chopped beef (or any other) liver, and top with watercress

Top: Spread bread with apple celery salad mixed with mayonnaise, and top with lettuce.

> nuts (any kind)
> olives
> whipped cream
> lettuce
> pineapple

Bottom: Cover fig bread with chopped nuts and olives mixed with whipped cream, and top with shredded lettuce.

Top: Cover bread with a well-drained pineapple slice and top with lettuce leaves.

> nuts (any kind)   lettuce leaves
> olives   American cheese
> green pepper   mustard
> mayonnaise

Bottom: Cover raisin bread with chopped nuts, olives, and green pepper, mixed in equal parts with mayonnaise, and top with lettuce.

Top: Cover bread with American cheese, spread with prepared mustard, and top with lettuce.

Onion Club Sandwiches

Bermuda onion
baked beans
lettuce leaves
hot dog
sweet-sour pickle

Bottom: Cover Boston brown bread with thinly sliced Bermuda onion, then with baked beans, and top with lettuce.

Top: Cover bread with hot dog (sliced lengthwise) then with thinly sliced sweet-sour pickle, and top with lettuce.

> Bermuda onion   mayonnaise
> prepared mustard   lettuce leaves
> dill pickles   ham (sliced)
> radishes

Bottom: Cover rye bread with thinly sliced Bermuda onion, spread with prepared mustard, then with thinly sliced dill pickles and sliced radishes, and top with lettuce dressed with mayonnaise.

Top: Cover bread with sliced ham, spread with prepared mustard, and top with lettuce.

Bermuda onion   tomato
pineapple   prepared mustard
lettuce   bacon
vinaigrette sauce

Bottom: Cover toast with thinly sliced Bermuda onion, dipped in vinaigrette sauce, then cover with a slice of well-drained pineapple, and top with lettuce.

Top: Cover toast with tomato slices, spread with prepared mustard, then with chopped, broiled bacon, and top with lettuce.

creamed onions
walnuts
lettuce
liver
bacon

Bottom: Cover toast with creamed onions mixed with chopped walnuts and top with shredded lettuce.

Top: Cover toast with a slice of liver, broiled very rare, then with broiled bacon, and top with lettuce leaves.

onion salad
cucumbers
lettuce leaves
tomato
bacon

Bottom: Spread onion salad on rye bread, then cover with sliced cucumbers, and top with lettuce.

Top: Cover bread with tomato slices, then with chopped, broiled bacon, and top with lettuce.

Peanut Butter Club Sandwiches
peanut butter
bacon
lettuce leaves
tomato
horseradish

Bottom: Spread toasted rye bread with peanut butter, then cover with fried bacon, and top with lettuce.

Top: Cover toast with tomato slices, spread with prepared horseradish, and top with lettuce.

peanut butter
banana
lettuce
orange marmalade

Bottom: Spread baking powder biscuit with peanut butter, then cover with
.a sliced banana, and top with lettuce leaves.

Top: Spread biscuit with orange marmalade and top with shredded lettuce.

peanut butter
celery stalks
tongue (sliced)
raisins
tomato
lettuce leaves

Bottom: Spread rye bread with peanut butter, then cover with small celery
stalks.

Top: Cover bread with sliced tongue, spread with chopped raisins, then
with tomato slices, and top with lettuce.

peanut butter
cranbery sauce
lettuce leaves
bacon
banana
watercress

Bottom: Spread baking powder biscuit with peanut butter, then with
cranberry sauce, and top with lettuce.

Top: Cover biscuit with crushed, broiled bacon, then with a sliced banana,
and top with watercress.

peanut butter
cream cheese
poppy seeds
lettuce leaves
pineapple
watercress

Bottom: Spread date bread with peanut butter, then with softened cream
cheese, sprinkle with poppy seeds, and top with lettuce.

Top: Cover bread with shredded pineapple and top with watercress.

peanut butter	lettuce leaves
dates	tomato
nuts (any kind)	Bermuda onion
mayonnaise	horseradish

Bottom: Spread orange bread with peanut butter, then cover with pitted chopped dates and nuts in equal parts, mixed with mayonnaise, and top with lettuce.

Top: Cover bread with tomato slices, then thinly sliced Bermuda onion, spread with horseradish, and top with lettuce.

peanut butter
ham (sliced)
lettuce
egg salad

Bottom: Spread toasted rye bread with peanut butter, then cover with ham, and top with shredded lettuce.

Top: Spread toast with egg salad and top with lettuce leaves

peanut butter
lettuce
green pepper
mayonnaise

tongue (sliced)
Swiss cheese
prepared mustard

Bottom: Spread raisin bread with peanut butter, then with shredded lettuce and chopped green pepper, mixed with mayonnaise.

Top: Cover bread with sliced, cold tongue, then with Swiss cheese, spread lightly with prepared mustard, and top with lettuce leaves.

peanut butter
olives
nuts (any kind)
lettuce leaves

tomato
bacon
watercress

Bottom: Spread pumpernickel bread with peanut butter, then cover with chopped olives and nuts, mixed in equal parts, and top with lettuce.

Top: Cover bread with tomato slices, then with chopped bacon, and top with shredded watercress.

peanut butter
olives (black)
shredded lettuce
American cheese
horseradish
dill pickle

Bottom: Spread toasted rye bread with peanut butter, then cover with chopped, pitted black olives, and top with shredded lettuce.

Top: Cover toast with American cheese, spread with prepared horseradish, top with thinly sliced dill pickle, then with shredded lettuce.

peanut butter
orange
watercress
celery greens
mayonnaise
lettuce leaves

Bottom: Spread cheese biscuit with peanut butter, then cover with a sliced, peeled, seedless orange, and top with chopped watercress.

Top: Cover biscuit with chopped celery greens mixed with mayonnaise and top with lettuce.

peanut butter
orange marmalade
lettuce leaves
American cheese
horseradish
watercress

Bottom: Spread nut bread with peanut butter, then with orange marmalade, and top with lettuce.

Top: Cover bread with American cheese, spread with prepared horseradish, and top with chopped watercress.

peanut butter
orange marmalade
watercress
Swiss cheese
prepared mustard

Bottom: Spread date nut bread with peanut butter, then with orange marmalade, and top with minced watercress.

Top: Cover bread with Swiss cheese, spread with prepared mustard, and top with minced watercress.

peanut butter
pimiento
green pepper rings
lettuce leaves
Swiss cheese
mustard

Bottom: Spread white bread with peanut butter, then cover with a whole slice of pimiento and green pepper rings, and top with lettuce.

Top: Cover bread with Swiss cheese, spread with prepared mustard, and top with lettuce.

peanut butter
pineapple

lettuce
mayonnaise
American cheese
prepared mustard

Bottom: Spread corn bread with peanut butter, then cover with pineapple slice, and top with shredded lettuce mixed with mayonnaise.

Top: Cover bread with American cheese, spread with prepared mustard, and top with lettuce leaves.

peanut butter
pineapple
lettuce leaves
Liederkranz cheese
caraway seeds

Bottom: Spread orange rye bread with peanut butter, then cover with shredded, well-drained pineapple, and top with lettuce.

Top: Cover bread with Liederkranz cheese, then sprinkle with caraway seeds, and top with lettuce.

peanut butter
prunes
lettuce leaves
pork (sliced)
sweet pickle

Bottom: Spread nut bread with peanut butter, then cover with cooked pitted prunes, and top with lettuce.

Top: Cover bread with sliced well-cooked pork, then with chopped sweet pickle, and top with lettuce.

peanut butter
red cole slaw
watercress
pineapple
lettuce leaves

Bottom: Spread nut bread with peanut butter, then cover with red cole slaw, and top with watercress.

Top: Cover bread with pineapple and top with lettuce.

peanut butter
sardines
lettuce
potato salad

Bottom: Spread rye bread with peanut butter, then cover with boneless sardines, and top with shredded lettuce.

Top: Spread bread with potato salad and top with lettuce leaves.

peanut butter
walnuts
lettuce
mayonnaise
cottage cheese
chives

Bottom: Spread rye or white bread with peanut butter, then cover with chopped walnuts, and top with shredded lettuce mixed with mayonnaise.
Top: Cover bread with rather dry cottage cheese, mixed with minced chives, and top with lettuce leaves.

peanut butter
watercress
cream cheese
celery
lettuce leaves

Bottom: Spread honey bread with peanut butter, then top with chopped watercress.
Top: Spread bread with cream cheese, mixed with chopped celery, and top with lettuce.

Pork Club Sandwiches
roast pork (sliced)
apple
watercress
green bean salad
lettuce leaves

Bottom: Spread rye bread with sliced roast pork, then with thin slices of pared, cored apple, and top with chopped watercress.
Top: Spread bread with green bean salad and top with lettuce.

roast pork (sliced)
apple sauce
lettuce
cabbage salad

Bottom: Cover rye bread with thinly sliced, well-cooked roast pork, then with rather thick apple sauce, and top with shredded lettuce.
Top: Spread bread with cabbage salad and top with lettuce leaves.

roast pork (sliced)
baked beans
lettuce leaves
tomato

prepared mustard

Bottom: Cover white or rye bread with sliced roast pork, then with cold baked beans, and top with lettuce.

Top: Cover bread with tomato slices, spread with prepared mustard, and top with lettuce.

roast pork (sliced)
green pepper rings
lettuce leaves
American cheese
prepared mustard
watercress

Bottom: Cover pumpernickel bread with cold, roasted pork, then with green pepper rings, and top with lettuce.

Top: Cover bread with American cheese, spread with prepared mustard, and top with watercress.

roast pork (sliced)   tomato
orange   prepared mustard
Burmuda onion   horseradish
lettuce leaves

Bottom: Cover rye bread with sliced roast pork, then with peeled orange slices, and top with thinly sliced Bermuda onion and lettuce.

Top: Cover bread with tomato slices, spread with prepared mustard and horseradish, mixed in equal parts, and top with lettuce.

roast pork (sliced)
pineapple
watercress
tomato
dill pickle
lettuce leaves

Bottom: Cover nut bread with sliced roast pork, then with well-drained pineapple slice, and top with watercress.

Top: Cover bread with tomato slices, then with thinly sliced dill pickle, and top with lettuce.

roast pork
Swiss cheese
lettuce leaves
potato salad

Bottom: Cover rye bread with roast pork, then with a thin slice of Swiss cheese, and top with lettuce.

Top: Spread bread with potato salad and top with lettuce.

Salmon Club Sandwiches
1 can salmon
lettuce leaves
4 slices bacon
broiled tomato slices
salt and pepper
cucumber

Bottom: Leave salmon in large pieces. Arrange salmon and lettuce leaves on toast. Top with 2 slices of bacon and a slice of tomato.
Top: Repeat the process and season to taste with salt and pepper. Top sandwich with a slice of cucumber.

salmon
sweet relish
lettuce
egg (hard-boiled)
apple

Bottom: Spread white or rye bread with a mixture (paste) of salmon and ground sweet relish and top with shredded lettuce.
Top: Cover bread with sliced hard-boiled egg, then with thinly sliced, pared, cored apple, and top with lettuce leaves.

salmon	heavy cream
walnuts	watercress
olives	American cheese
celery	

Bottom: Cover toast with a mixture made of equal parts of salmon, chopped walnuts, olives, and minced celery, mixed with a little seasoned heavy cream, and top with shredded watercress.
Top: Cover toast with American cheese and top with watercress.

Salmon Salad Club Sandwiches
salmon salad
nuts (any kind)
lettuce
egg (hard-boiled)
mayonnaise
ketchup

Bottom: Spread toast with salmon salad, then top with chopped nuts and lettuce leaves.
Top: Cover toast with sliced, hard-boiled egg, then top with shredded lettuce, mixed with mayonnaise and a little ketchup.

salmon salad
spinach
lettuce leaves
tomato
prepared mustard
bacon

Bottom: Spread white bread with salmon salad, then cover with chopped, raw spinach, and top with lettuce.
Top: Cover bread with tomato slices, spread with mustard, then with broiled bacon, and top with lettuce.

salmon salad
watercress
asparagus tips
tomato
prepared mustard
lettuce leaves

Bottom: Spread toast with salmon salad, and top with watercress.
Top: Cover toast with asparagus tips, then with tomato slices, spread with prepared mustard, and top with lettuce.

Sardine Club Sandwiches
sardines
American cheese
lettuce
shrimp salad

Bottom: Cover toasted whole wheat bread with boneless sardines, then with American cheese, and top with shredded lettuce.
Top: Spread toast with shrimp salad and top with lettuce leaves.

sardines	cucumber
anchovy paste	mayonnaise
watercress	tomato
bacon	

Bottom: Spread rye bread with a thin film of anchovy paste, then cover with boneless sardines, and top with watercress.
Top: Cover bread with chopped bacon, then with chopped, pared cucumber mixed with a little mayonnaise, then with tomato slices, and top with watercress.

sardines
bacon
lettuce leaves

tomato
sweet relish

Bottom: Cover rye bread with boneless sardines, then with broiled bacon, and top with lettuce.

Top: Cover bread with tomato slices, then with chopped, well-drained sweet relish, and top with lettuce.

sardines
Bermuda onion
lettuce leaves
Swiss cheese
horseradish

Bottom: Cover whole wheat bread with boneless sardines, then with a thin slice of broiled Bermuda onion, and top with lettuce.

Top: Cover bread with Swiss cheese, spread with prepared horseradish, and top with lettuce.

sardines
egg (hard-boiled)
ketchup
mayonnaise
lettuce leaves
scallions
radishes

Bottom: Cover white or rye bread with boneless sardines, then with sliced, hard-boiled egg, dotted with ketchup, mayonnaise, and top with lettuce.

Top: Cover bread with scallions, then with sliced radishes, and top with lettuce.

sardines
eggs (scrambled)
lettuce leaves
tomato
prepared mustard

Bottom: Cover whole wheat bread with boneless sardines, then with cold scrambled eggs, and top with lettuce.

Top: Cover bread with tomato slices, spread with prepared mustard, and top with lettuce.

sardines
green pepper
pimiento
ketchup
lettuce leaves
salami
prepared mustard

Bottom: Cover white bread with a mixture of equal parts of mashed sardines, chopped green pepper, and pimiento, blended with ketchup, and top with lettuce.

Top: Cover bread with sliced salami, spread with prepared mustard, and top with lettuce.

    sardines
    grilled tomato slices
    lettuce leaves
    cucumber or onion

Bottom: Cover a layer of toast with sardines, then top with tomato slices. Cover with lettuce leaves.

Top: Repeat the process from the lower layer, adding either broiled cucumbers or onion rings to this layer.

    sardines
    horseradish
    lettuce
    pimiento
    shrimp salad

Bottom: Cover rye bread with a mixture of equal parts of mashed sardines and prepared horseradish and top with shredded lettuce mixed with chopped pimiento.

Top: Spread bread with shrimp salad and top with lettuce leaves.

    sardines   Bermuda onion
    ketchup   pineapple
    egg (hard-boiled)   watercress
    lettuce leaves

Bottom: Cover rye bread with boneless sardines, then with a little ketchup and sliced hard-boiled egg, and top with lettuce.

Top: Cover bread with thinly sliced Bermuda onion, then with a slice of pineapple, and top with watercress.

    sardines
    lettuce
    vinaigrette sauce
    tomato
    anchovies

Bottom: Cover white bread with sardines, then top with shredded lettuce mixed with vinaigrette sauce.

Top: Cover bread with tomato slices, then with anchovies and top with lettuce leaves.

    sardines
    nuts (any kind)
    mayonnaise

lettuce leaves
crabmeat salad

Bottom: Cover orange bread with boneless sardines, then with chopped nuts mixed with a little mayonnaise, and top with lettuce.
Top: Spread bread with crabmeat salad and top with lettuce.

sardines	lettuce leaves
nuts (any kind)	salami
black olives	horseradish
mayonnaise	tomato

Bottom: Cover rye bread with a paste made of equal parts of mashed sardines, chopped nuts, and black olives, blended with a little mayonnaise, and top with lettuce.
Top: Cover bread with salami, spread with horseradish, then with tomato slices, and top with lettuce.

sardines
olives
lettuce
tomato
mayonnaise
cucumber

Bottom: Cover white or rye bread with boneless sardines, then with chopped, pitted olives and top with shredded lettuce.
Top: Cover bread with sliced tomatoes, spread with mayonnaise, and top with thinly sliced cucumber and lettuce leaves.

sardines	prepared mustard
onion	dill pickle
watercress	lettuce leaves
Swiss cheese	

Bottom: Cover whole wheat bread with boneless sardines, then with chopped onion, and top with watercress.
Top: Cover bread with Swiss cheese, spread with prepared mustard, then with thinly sliced dill pickle, and top with lettuce.

sardines
pineapple
lettuce leaves
tomato
anchovy paste

Bottom: Cover whole wheat bread with mashed sardines, then with shredded, well-drained pineapple, and top with lettuce.
Top: Cover bread with tomato slices, spread with anchovy paste, and top with lettuce.

sardines
tomato
lettuce leaves
Bermuda onion
caviar

Bottom: Cover rye bread with boneless sardines, then with tomato slices, and top with lettuce.

Top: Cover bread with thinly sliced Bermuda onion, then with caviar, and top with lettuce.

sardines
tomato
horseradish
lettuce leaves
baked beans

Bottom: Cover whole wheat bread with boneless sardines, then with tomato slices, spread with prepared horseradish, and top with lettuce.

Top: Cover bread with cold seasoned baked beans, and top with lettuce.

sardines
tomato
mayonnaise
lettuce leaves
cucumber salad
Bermuda onion

Bottom: Cover rye bread with boneless sardines, then with tomato slices, spread with a little mayonnaise, and top with lettuce.

Top: Cover bread with cucumber salad, then with a thin slice of Bermuda onion, and top with lettuce.

sardines
watercress
mayonnaise
cream cheese
lettuce leaves
caraway seeds

Bottom: Cover nut bread with boneless sardines, then with chopped watercress mixed with mayonnaise.

Top: Spread bread with cream cheese, sprinkle with caraway seeds, and top with lettuce.

Shrimp Salad Club Sandwiches
shrimp salad
cucumber

watercress
tongue(sliced)
green pepper rings
lettuce leaves

Bottom: Spread Boston brown bread with shrimp salad mixed with cubed cucumber and top with chopped watercress.

Top: Cover bread with sliced, cold cooked tongue, then with green pepper rings, and top with lettuce.

shrimp salad
nuts (any kind)
lettuce leaves
American cheese
horseradish

Bottom: Spread rye bread with shrimp salad mixed with chopped nuts and top with lettuce.

Top: Cover bread with American cheese, spread with prepared horseradish, and top with lettuce.

shrimp salad
pineapple
lettuce leaves
tomato
ketchup

Bottom: Spread toast with shrimp salad, mixed in equal parts with well-drained shredded pineapple, and top with lettuce.

Top: Cover toast with tomato slices, spread with ketchup, and top with lettuce.

shrimp salad   dill pickle
tomato   prepared mustard
lettuce leaves   green pepper rings
veal (sliced)

Bottom: Spread pumpernickel bread with shrimp salad, cover with tomato slices, and top with lettuce.

Top: Cover bread with sliced, cold cooked veal, then with thinly sliced dill pickle, spread with prepared mustard, cover with green pepper rings, and top with lettuce.

Tomato Salad Club Sandwich
tomato salad
bacon
lettuce leaves

American cheese
cole slaw
watercress

Bottom: Spread rye bread with tomato salad, cover with broiled or fried bacon, and top with lettuce.

Top: Cover bread with American cheese, then with cole slaw, and top with watercress.

Tuna Club Sandwiches

tuna fish	lettuce leaves
tomato	anchovies
prepared mustard	**red cole slaw**
dill pickles	

Bottom: Cover rye bread with tuna fish and sliced tomato, thinly spread with prepared mustard, then thinly sliced dill pickles, and top with lettuce.

Top: Cover bread with anchovies, then with red cole slaw, and top with lettuce.

Tuna Salad Club Sandwich

tuna salad	horseradish
pimiento	green pepper rings
watercress	lettuce leaves
egg (hard-boiled)	

Bottom: Spread rye bread with tuna salad, then cover with chopped red pimiento, and top with chopped watercress.

Top: Cover bread with sliced, hard-boiled egg, dotted with well-drained, prepared horseradish, and then with green pepper rings, and top with lettuce.

Vegetable Salad Club Sandwich
vegetable salad
watercress
asparagus tips
red cabbage
mayonnaise or ketchup

Bottom: Spread white or rye bread with vegetable salad and top with chopped watercress.

Top: Cover bread with asparagus tips, then with finely shredded red cabbage mixed with mayonnaise or ketchup.

Cold Sandwiches

The following sandwich combinations are proven winners, but we strongly encourage you to do some creative tinkering. Sandwiches are rather personal affairs, and unless an extremely delicate balance is required we've left the exact proportions up to you. Suggestions for specific breads are made where it would highlight a particular flavor. Also, keep in mind the chapter on "Fillings and Salads"; many of these recipes may stimulate your imagination and inspire ever new and more interesting combinations.

Avocado Sandwich
avocado slices
crisp bacon
spinach leaves
cream cheese, pimiento, and walnut filling
lemon juice

Sprinkle the avocado slices with lemon juice to prevent browning. Spread the cream cheese, pimiento, and walnut filling on toast. Cover with avocado slices, bacon, and spinach leaves. Top with another slice of toast.

Canadian Cheese and Apple Sandwich
grated American or Cheddar cheese
1 apple
mayonnaise
lettuce

Pare and core the apple, and slice so that it may be placed on bread. After putting the apple on the bread, sprinkle it with grated cheese mixed with mayonnaise. Top with crisp lettuce leaves.

Carrot, Watercress, and Onion Sandwich
carrot filling
watercress
sliced Bermuda onion

Spread carrot filling on wheat toast. Cover with watercress and sliced onion. Top with toast.

Cheese and Caviar Sandwich
grated American or Cheddar cheese mushrooms
caviar salt and pepper
onion powder paprika
white sauce

Sprinkle onion powder over toast and spread with the caviar. Over this pour the white sauce, into which has been stirred equal parts grated cheese and ground mushrooms. Season to taste with salt and pepper, and pour over the caviar on the toast. Dust with paprika.

Cheese Dream Sandwich
Swiss cheese
prepared mustard
minced onion

Between the slices of bread place the thinly sliced Swiss cheese. Spread cheese with mustard and then with the minced onion. Garnish with a slice of tomato.

Cheese and Fried Bacon Sandwich
sliced American, Edam, or Cheddar cheese
2 slices crisp bacon
lettuce leaves

Cover bread with the sliced cheese. Over this place the bacon and top with lettuce leaves.

Cheese and Peanut Butter Sandwich
American, Edam, or Cheddar cheese
peanut butter

Spread peanut butter on bread. Cover this with cheese.
Variation:
1. Use apple butter in place of peanut butter.

123

Cheese and Tomato Sandwich
thinly sliced American, Edam, or Cheddar cheese
thin slices tomato
lettuce leaves

Cover bread with the cheese, then with tomato slices, and top with crisp lettuce leaves. Cut from corner to corner, making two triangular sandwiches.

Cottage Cheese and Marmalade Sandwich
cottage cheese
salt and pepper
onion powder
lettuce leaves
marmalade (orange, strawberry, etc.)

Spread brown bread generously with well-drained cottage cheese seasoned to taste with salt, pepper, and onion powder. Top with lettuce leaves. Spread the other slice of bread with marmalade and adjust it over the first slice. Cut from corner to corner both ways.

Cream Cheese and Apple Sandwich

In this sandwich, large slices of apples, not bread, are used.
cheese
ground nuts (any kind)
lemon juice
sliced apples
lettuce leaves

Rub lemon juice over apple slices to prevent browning. Mix the cream cheese with the nuts and spread over the apple slices. Adjust together and place on lettuce leaves. Garnish with an olive and sweet relish.
Variations:
1. Mix cream cheese with chopped ripe olives.
2. Mix cream cheese with chopped green pepper.
3. Mix cream cheese with watercress.
4. Mix cream cheese with chives.

Cream Cheese and Asparagus Tips Sandwich
cream cheese
fresh, cooked asparagus tips

Spread the cream cheese over slices of bread, cover with a row of asparagus tips, and top with a slice of bread. Cut diagonally. Garnish with a cup of lettuce leaves filled with cole slaw sprinkled with minced beets.

Cream Cheese and Cucumber Sandwich

cream cheese
salt
coarsely ground black pepper
Tabasco sauce
lettuce leaves (optional)
cucumber
mayonnaise

To the cream cheese add enough mayonnaise to make a mixture of spreadable consistency. Season with salt, pepper, and Tabasco sauce. Spread between two slices of bread with or without lettuce leaves. Cut diagonally and on top of bread place cucumber slices afixed with a toothpick.

Cream Cheese and Grape Nuts Sandwich

cream cheese
grape nuts
1 tsp. ground blanched almonds
salt and pepper
minced pimiento

To 3 parts cream cheese add 1 part grape nuts and the almonds. Salt and pepper to taste and blend thoroughly. Spread mixture on slices of bread and cover with minced pimiento. Garnish with a small stick of pineapple.

Cream Cheese and Green Pepper Sandwich

8 oz. cream cheese
2 hard-boiled eggs
1 Tbs. minced pimiento
2 Tbs. minced green pepper
salt and pepper
lettuce leaves

Rice or sieve the eggs and combine with the cream cheese, pimiento, and green pepper. Season to taste with salt and pepper. Mix well. Spread between two slices of bread covered with lettuce. Garnish with a section of orange dipped in vinaigrette sauce placed on a piece of lettuce.

Cream Cheese and Honey Sandwich

cream cheese
chopped nuts
honey

Add enough honey to the cream cheese to make a spreadable mixture. Sprinkle with the chopped nuts and serve open-faced.

Cream Cheese and Jelly Sandwich

cream cheese
jelly

Spread cream cheese on one slice of bread and spread any kind of jelly on the other. Fold togther and cut from corner to corner to make four small triangular sandwiches. Garnish with shredded pineapple placed on a crisp lettuce leaf.

Variations:
1. Use marmalade in place of jelly.
2. Use two different kinds of bread.

Cream Cheese and Olive Sandwich

cream cheese
chopped olives (any kind)
lettuce leaves

After spreading cream cheese over a slice of bread, sprinkle with finely chopped olives. Cover with crisp lettuce leaves.

Cream Cheese and Sardine Sandwich

cream cheese
well-drained sardines
minced olives (any kind)
vinaigrette sauce
anchovy paste

Combine 1 part cream cheese, 1 part sardines with 2 parts minced olives. Season with salt and pepper to taste and add enough vinaigrette sauce to make the mixture spreadable. Spread between two slices of bread that have been thinly spread with anchovy paste.

Dixie Ambrosia

peanut butter
apple slices
lemon juice
strawberry preserves
banana slices
cinnamon

Rub lemon juice over the apple slices to prevent browning. Spread peanut butter on raisin bread and cover with strawberry preserves. Over this place the apple and banana slices. Sprinkle with cinnamon.

Greek Salad Sandwich

feta cheese
tomatoes

lettuce
onion
anchovies (optional)
oil and vinegar
black olives

Chop the above ingredients as for a salad and sprinkle with the oil and vinegar. Cut about ¼ inch from the top of a piece of pita bread to give access to the pocket of the bread and stuff with the salad.

Ham and Brie Sandwich

thinly sliced ham
Brie cheese

Spread the cheese on thinly sliced rye toast. Cover with 1 or 2 slices of ham. Top with toast.

Liederkranz and Tomato Sandwich

Liederkranz
anchovy butter
ketchup
horseradish
sliced tomato

Spread slices of rye or pumpernickel bread with anchovy butter and then with Liederkranz. Cover the cheese with a thin layer of ketchup mixed with horseradish. Over this, place the slices of tomato. Garnish with black olives.
Variations:
1. Substitute **garlic butter** for the anchovy butter.
2. Substitute **mustard butter** for the anchovy butter.
3. Use any combination of the above butters with the anchovy butter.

Logs

sliced ham
sliced cheese (any kind)
prepared mustard

Cut off the crust of bread and flatten the bread lightly with a rolling pin. Place a few slices of ham and cheese on the bread. Cover with a layer of mustard and roll the bread up (like a jelly roll). Use a toothpick to hold it closed, and put an olive through the top of the toothpick.

Lox and Cream Cheese Sandwich

lox
cream cheese

Lox is usually thought of as an appetizer, but when sliced very thin and placed on a toasted bagel or rye bread with cream cheese, it becomes a very filling and tasty sandwich.

Variations:
1. Try with slices of either tomato, cucumber, or Bermuda onion or with all of these.
2. Substitute whitefish for the lox.
3. Substitute **tuna salad** for the lox.

Parmesan Cheese and Tomato Paste Sandwich
3 Tbs. grated Parmesan cheese
1 Tbs. ketchup
1 Tbs. tomato paste
minced peanuts
lettuce
4 slices broiled tomatoes

To the Parmasan cheese add ketchup and tomato paste. Spread on a slice of toast and top with minced peanuts. Cover this with lettuce leaves and a slice of toast. Cut from corner to corner to make four triangular sandwiches and top each section with a slice of broiled tomato.

Roquefort Cheese, Caviar, Egg, and Tomato Sandwich
creamed Roquefort cheese
sliced tomato
caviar
lettuce leaves
hard-boiled eggs

Arrange the cheese on one half of slice of rye bread and the slices of tomato on the other half. On another slice of either rye bread or pumpernickel bread arrange lettuce spread with caviar on one half and the chopped hard-boiled egg on the other half. Leave open faced and garnish with a small cup of lettuce filled with finely chopped onion sprinkled with paprika.

Roquefort Cheese and Chicken Sandwich
Roquefort cheese
thin slices of cooked chicken
mustard butter
slices of tomato

Spread two slices of bread with mustard butter. On one slice, place the cheese and the slices of chicken. Top with a slice of tomato. Cover with the other slice of bread.

Swiss Cheese and Asparagus Sandwich
thinly sliced Swiss cheese
cooked asparagus tips
lettuce leaves

Place asparagus tips on the bread and cover with lettuce. Top with Swiss cheese and a slice of bread.

Swiss Chess, Asparagus, and Bacon Sandwich

thinly sliced Swiss cheese
crisp bacon
cooked asparagus tips
prepared musard (optional)

Arrange asparagus tips on a slice of bread covered with lettuce leaves. Top the asparagus with bacon slices, then Swiss cheese spread with mustard if desired. Cover with another slice of bread and garnish with a slice of tomato.

Swiss Cheese, Corned Beef, and Bologna Sandwich

Swiss scheese
thinly sliced corned beef
thinly sliced bologna
shredded lettuce

Arrange alternate layers of Swiss cheese, shredded lettuce, then corned beef and shredded lettuce. Top with the bologna and more shredded lettuce. Cut diagonally and top each part with a slice of dill pickle.

Swiss Cheese and Cole Slaw Sandwich

thinly sliced Swiss cheese
cole slaw

Spread cole slaw evenly between two slices of bread and top with the Swiss cheese. Garnish with one olive and a radish.

Swiss Cheese and Crabmeat Sandwich

thinly sliced Swiss cheese
crabmeat salad

Spread the crabmeat salad, topped with Swiss cheese, between two slices of toast. Garnish with an olive and a slice of lemon.

Swiss Cheese and Egg Sandwich

Swiss cheese
sliced hard-boiled egg
lettuce leaves
prepared mustard

Place the Swiss cheese between two slices of bread which have been spread with mustard. Top the cheese with the hard-boiled egg and cover with lettuce leaves.

Variations:
1. Substitute **mustard butter** for the mustard.
2. Substitute **horseradish butter** for the mustard.

Swiss Cheese and Ham Sandwich

thinly sliced Swiss cheese
thinly sliced ham
prepared mustard or **mustard butter**
lettuce leaves

On a slice of bread that has been spread with mustard or mustard butter, arrange Swiss cheese. Cover with crisp lettuce leaves and top that with ham. Cover with a slice of bread also spread with mustard. Garnish with a little horseradish on a leaf of lettuce.

Variation:

1. Substitute for the ham, liverwurst, potato salad, cold cooked pork, thinly sliced roast beef, salami, tongue, sliced tomatoes, or thinly sliced turkey garnished with cranberry sauce.

Hot Sandwiches

Although most of the recipes for the following hot sandwiches need no elaboration, a few tips are worth keeping in mind.

When grilling a sandwich, use a frying pan with a lid. Heat a small amount of butter, oil, or bacon fat at a medium temperature, and when the pan is hot—not smoking—put in the sandwich and put on the lid. After 3 or 4 minutes use a spatula to lift a corner of the bread to see if it's brown, and if it is, turn the sandwich over carefully (using your fingers to balance the sandwich while turning with the spatula) and brown the other side.

Broilers, ovens, and toaster ovens all work well for toasting breads, melting cheese, and otherwise heating up your sandwich materials, though a toaster oven is your best bet in the summer.

Bacon, Lettuce, and Tomato
3 slices crisp bacon
lettuce leaves
sliced tomato
mayonnaise (optional)
basil (optional)

Place bacon on a slice of wheat toast spread with mayonnaise if desired. Cover with crisp lettuce and sliced tomato. The tomato may be raw or broiled with the bacon and sprinkled with basil if desired.

Bagel and Muenster Cheese Sandwich

cream cheese
tomato slices
onion
Muenster cheese

Toast a bagel and place the slices of tomato on each half. Top with slices of onion and Muenster cheese. Place under broiler until the cheese melts. Serve open faced.

Baked Beans Cheesewich

baked beans
1 slice American or Cheddar cheese
2 strips crisp bacon

On a slice of toast spread heated baked beans. Top with a slice of cheese and place under broiler until the cheese melts. Cover with bacon and crisp lettuce, and top with toast.

Baked Beans Rarebit Sandwich

Welsh rarebit
baked beans
grated onion
prepared mustard or ketchup
salt and pepper

Prepare Welsh rarebit and spread thickly on both slices of bread. Mash the baked beans, then heat and season to taste with salt, pepper, mustard or ketchup, and the grated onion. Put the 2 slices of bread together, cheese side in, with a filling of the baked bean mixture between. Toast or brown in a frying pan. Serve at once.

Broiled Tomato Sandwich

1 tomato
oil or bacon fat
lettuce leaves
salt and pepper
basil (optional)

Cut a tomato into thick slices. Season with salt, pepper, and basil to taste and dip in the oil or bacon fat. Broil on both sides and put between slices of toast covered with crisp lettuce leaves.

Cape Cod Sandwich

crabmeat salad
American cheese

Spread a generous layer of crabmeat salad (not too moist) over a slice of toast. Cover with a slice of cheese and broil until cheese melts. Cover with last piece of toast and serve right away.

Chicken Briarcliff Manor Sandwich

hot chicken slices
ham slices
broiled tomato slices
lettuce leaves

Arrange slices of chicken and ham on toast. Cover with crisp lettuce and top with a thick slice of broiled tomato.

Cream Tuna Sandwich

anchovy paste
creamed tuna fish
lettuce leaves
broiled tomato slices

Spread toast with anchovy paste and heap with creamed tuna fish. Top with lettuce leaves, broiled tomato, and the second slice of toast, also spread with anchovy paste.

Denver Sandwich

1 lb. chopped raw ham
2 eggs
1 tsp. onion powder
salt and pepper
1 Tbs. bacon fat

Mix chopped (not ground) ham, 2 eggs, and the onion powder together. Heat the bacon fat in a frying pan and cook the mixture in it for 5 minutes, stirring occasionally. Serve on toast while still hot. Add salt and pepper to taste.

Fish Cake Sandwich

1 or 2 fish cakes
tomato sauce

Fry fish cakes and place them between 2 slices of bread or a roll. Cover with the tomato sauce. Garnish with black olives.

French Cheese Sandwich

well-drained cottage cheese
heavy cream or evaporated milk
1 loaf French bread
1 egg
milk

salt and pepper
nutmeg
butter
jelly

Mix the cottage cheese with enough heavy cream or evaporated milk to get a thick but spreadable consistency. Spread on the French bread. Slightly beat the egg and dilute with milk. Season with salt, pepper, and nutmeg, and dip the entire piece of bread in the egg mixture. Fry in butter until golden brown, cut crosswise, and serve with a spoonful of jelly in the center.

Fried Egg and Green Pepper Sandwich

1 egg
1 Tbs. chopped green pepper

Beat an egg slightly and add the green pepper. Fry on both sides and serve on toast or a roll.

Variations:

1. Fried Egg and Onion Sandwich. Proceed as above but substitute onion fried in butter for the pepper.
2. Fried Egg and Tomato Sandwich. Proceed as above but substitute 1 tablespoon stewed tomato for the pepper.

Fried Salami and Cheese Sandwich

salami (sliced)
cream cheese

Fry the salami for a few minutes until hot. Spread the cream cheese on bread and place the hot salami on the cheese.

Grilled Salami Sandwich

salami (sliced)
slices of tomato
Swiss cheese
cooking oil

Place the salami in the frying pan for a few minutes to heat. Place the cooked salami, tomato slices, and cheese on rye bread. Put the cooking oil in the frying pan and heat. When the pan is hot, put in the sandwich, and brown on both sides. When browned, the cheese should be melted. Remove from pan and serve.

Ham and Egg Sandwich

1 slice ham
1 egg

Fry a slice of ham on one side. When done, turn it over and break the egg on top of the ham. When the egg begins to harden, turn the ham and egg over and cook the egg on the other side. Remove and place between slices of whole wheat toast.

Ham and Swiss Cheese Sandwich
Swiss cheese
2 pieces broiled ham
slice of tomato
prepared mustard

On one slice of bread place Swiss cheese spread with mustard between 2 slices of broiled ham. Top with a slice of tomato and cover with bread. Place in broiler or toaster oven until bread is toasted.

Hamburger
ground beef
chopped onions
bread crumbs
minced garlic
Worcestershire sauce
chopped mushrooms (optional)

Mix the above ingredients together and press lightly into shape. Hamburgers may be fried, broiled, or cooked in the oven. No fat is needed in the pan when frying. Serve on toasted round roll.

Variations:

1. Top hamburgers with fresh lettuce leaves and slices of tomato.
2. Top with raw sliced onions.
3. Condiments such as prepared mustard, mayonnaise, ketchup, and relishes are good on hamburgers.
4. Sauté onions and top the cooked hamburger with them before serving.
5. Sauté mushrooms and green pepper and top cooked hamburger with them.
6. Top cooked hamburger with a thinly sliced piece of boiled ham.
7. Cheeseburger. Top cooked hamburger with American cheese, bleu cheese, or Cheddar cheese and place under broiler until cheese melts.
8. Cover cooked hamburger with 2 slices of bacon and then with cheese. Place hamburger under broiler until cheese melts.
9. Cover cooked hamburger with cheese and broil until cheese melts. Top with highly spiced tomato or pizza sauce.

Hot Corned Beef Sandwich
thinly sliced corned beef
horseradish sauce

Place hot corned beef on rye bread spread with horseradish sauce and put in a toaster oven (or steam it if a steamer is available).

Variations:

1. Replace horseradish sauce with **cole slaw** and **Russian dressing**.
2. Use hot pastrami instead of corned beef.

Hot Dogs (Frankfurters)

Hot dogs may be fried, steamed, or boiled. When cooking, make sure to cut slightly into the surface of the meat with a knife (slits at intervals of an inch or one long line down the side). Serve on a hot dog roll or a long Italian roll.

Variations:

1. Cover the hot dog with hot sauerkraut before serving.
2. Relish, ketchup, onions, and prepared mustard are all excellent condiments with hot dogs.

Hot Dog, Bologna, and Potato Salad

hot dog
bologna
potato salad

Just as the hot dog is done cooking, wrap it with a few slices of very thinly cut bologna. Return it to the frying pan or steamer for a few minutes more. Remove and place on a roll. Top with potato salad.

Hot Dog, Cheese, and Bacon

hot dog
2 slices crisp bacon
American or cheddar cheese, sliced thin

After the hot dog is cooked, place it in the roll and place a piece of bacon on either side of it. Cover with the cheese and place in a broiler until the cheese melts.

Hot Dog and Chili

hot dog
chili

After the hot dog is cooked, place it on a roll and cover it with the chili which has already been heated.

Variation:

1. Cover the chili with thinly sliced cheese and broil until cheese melts.

Hot Dog, Fried Onions, and Peppers

hot dog
chopped onions
chopped peppers
cooking oil

Slice the hot dog down the middle without separating the top from the bottom. In a skillet, sauté the onions and peppers in the oil until almost done. Put the hot dog in the skillet and cook. When done, place hot dog on a roll with the sautéed onions and peppers.

Hot Roast Beef Sandwich

sliced roast beef
brown gravy

Place a slice of bread in the center of the plate, cover with hot roast beef, and pour rich brown gravy over the meat. Eaten with mashed potatoes, this is a very filling sandwich.

Variations:

1. Hot Chicken Sandwich. Slice chicken meat thin and serve in the same manner as the roast beef. Use gravy made from the chicken stock.
2. Hot Turkey Sandwich. Prepare in the same manner as the chicken sandwich, but substitute hot turkey slices for the chicken.

Lamb Sandwich

sliced lamb
mustard butter

Spread the mustard butter on a slice of bread and place the hot lamb slices on top. Garnish with a sprig of fresh mint. Serve open faced.

Liver and Bacon Sandwich

2 slices uncooked bacon
beef liver
½ hard-boiled egg
slice of onion
garlic (optional)
½ tsp. horseradish
1 tsp. sour cream

Fry the bacon until crisp; drain off nearly all the fat and fry the beef liver in the remaining fat (almost nothing). Put the bacon, liver, and hard-boiled egg through a food chopper with the onion, garlic, horseradish, and sour cream. Spread thickly on rye bread. Garnish with a piece of gherkin and a sprig of watercress.

Open-Faced Tuna Salad Sandwich

tuna salad
Swiss cheese
2 slices tomato
sliced onion

Heat an English muffin and cover with the tuna salad. Over this, place the tomato slices and the onion and top with Swiss Cheese. Place under the broiler or in the oven until the cheese melts.

Pita with Cheese Sandwich

½ sliced or chopped tomato

grated cheese (any kind)

Open a piece of pita bread and stuff with the grated cheese and tomatoes. Bake in a medium oven until the cheese melts.

Variation:

1. Use slices of crisp, chopped bacon mixed in with the cheese and tomatoes.

Pork Sandwich

hot roast pork slices
mustard butter

Heat the pork and serve on 1 slice of bread spread with mustard butter. Garnish with a thick slice of apple fried in butter until brown on both sides.

Reuben

corned beef, sliced thin
Swiss cheese
sauerkraut
Russian dressing

Place two slices of rye bread on a hot, greased skillet. Cover the bread with corned beef, then sauerkraut. Spoon Russian dressing over the meat and cover with Swiss cheese. Cover the pan and heat until the cheese melts. May be served open-faced or closed.

Sardine and Egg Sandwich

sardines
grated American cheese
1 hard-boiled egg
white sauce
prepared mustard

Mash the sardines with a little mustard and spread on toast. Sprinkle chopped hard-boiled egg on the sardines and cover with white sauce. Over this, generously sprinkle grated cheese and then brown the sandwich in the broiler. Serve open-faced at once.

Scrambled Egg Sandwich

Scrambled eggs may be enjoyed on toast with no other element or may be eaten in combination with other foods.

Scrambled Eggs and Anchovy Butter

1 scrambled egg
anchovy butter
2 slices crisp bacon

Spread the scrambled egg on a slice of toast spread with anchovy butter. Cover with 2 slices of bacon and top with another slice of toast. Cut the sandwich in quarters.

Soyburgers

1 cup cooked soybeans	3 Tbs. chopped onions
2 Tbs. oil	2 eggs, beaten
1 cup boiled rice	chopped celery (optional)
sesame seeds	chopped pepper (optional)

Sauté the onions, celery, and pepper in oil. Remove from pan and mix with the rice, eggs, and soybeans. Season to taste with salt and pepper or soy sauce. Shape into patties and press into sesame seeds. Sauté the patties in oil until golden brown, or bake in oven at 350° for 20 to 25 minutes.

Variations:

1. Soyburgers may be seasoned with basil or garlic powder.
2. Any variations listed for **hamburgers** would be appropriate with soyburgers.

Swiss Cheese and Pear Sandwich

sliced Swiss cheese
1 pear, pared, cored, and sliced
sugar
cinnamon

Toast the bread. Place cheese on toast and arrange pear slices over the cheese. Mix 2 parts sugar to 1 part cinnamon and sprinkle over the pears. Broil until lightly browned.

Tofu, Sour Cream, and Dill Sandwich

tofu	sour cream
chopped onions	dill
chopped tomatoes	rosemary
Worcestershire sauce	thyme

Cut the tofu into cubes and leave in the refrigerator with something heavy on it to press some of the liquid out. Press for about 12 hours for best results. Fry the tofu in butter until crisp. Season with a dash of Worcestershire sauce, thyme, and rosemary. Add the tomatoes and onions and sauté with the tofu until they are just barely limp. Take off the heat and stir in the sour cream, just enough to cover everything, and add dill to taste. Serve hot or cold in pita bread.

Tomato Buns Sandwich

peanut butter
mayonnaise

tomato
2 slices bacon
soft round roll

Split round soft roll three-quarters open and spread generously with peanut butter, then with mayonnaise. Broil the bacon and slices of tomato and place in the roll. Garnish with sprigs of watercress and one large black olive.

Tongue Sandwich
cold cooked tongue
meat or chicken broth
steamed spinach
egg sauce

Heat cold cooked tongue in meat or chicken broth, or in brown gravy. Place 2 or 3 slices on a piece of bread. Cover with a thick layer of steamed spinach, and over that pour hot egg sauce.

Wall Street Sandwich
2 slices bacon
American or Cheddar cheese
cayenne
lettuce leaves
sliced tomato
salt and pepper

On 1 slice of toast place a slice of cheese, then add a dash of cayenne and top with 2 slices of uncooked bacon. Toast under a broiler until the cheese melts and the bacon is cooked. On a second slice of toast arrange the lettuce and tomato and season with salt and pepper. Serve as a hot and cold, open-faced sandwich arrangement, garnished with pickle relish.

Western Sandwich
1 egg
1 Tbs. chopped chicken
1 Tbs. chopped pimiento
horseradish butter

Beat an egg slightly and add the chopped chicken and chopped pimiento. Fry in butter on both sides and serve on toast with horseradish butter. An interesting garnish for this sandwich is a large pitted black olive stuffed with cream cheese mixed with chopped walnuts.
Variation:
1. Add a broiled tomato and a leaf of crisp lettuce to the sandwich before covering.

140

Oversized Sandwiches

If club sandwiches are meals unto themselves, then the oversized sandwiches we've collected are feasts unto themselves, capable of satisfying even the most insatiable appetites. Heroic dimensions aside, though, the following hoagies, cheese steaks, and grinders are deliciously satisfying creations—even, we might say, addictive.

Hoagies, heroes, grinders, subs, zeps—the names are almost as colorful as the sandwiches themselves. Both the names and the sandwiches vary from one part of the country to the next, but the basic premise remains the same: a long roll filled with lunch meats, cheese, vegetables, spices, dressings, lots of inspiration, and more than a little soul. (The only limiting factor is the length of the roll, and some hoagies have been worthy of the **Guinness Book of World Records**.) A hot variation on the theme is the oven grinder, which, as its name implies, is put in the oven to melt the cheese and otherwise heat things up. The popular Philadelphia version of the steak sandwich—the cheese steak—has spawned countless variations, including a number of meatless versions that substitute eggplant or mushrooms for steak. The steaks themselves can be purchased at the frozen foods section or meat counter of most grocery stores; particularly convenient are the frozen versions that come already sliced and separated into individual servings.

American or Regular Hoagie

3 slices salami	chopped or sliced onions
3 slices bologna	oil

3 slices American cheese	oregano
1 slice ham	pepper
shredded lettuce	hot peppers (optional)
3 slices tomato	

Slice a long roll lengthwise without severing the top from the bottom. Inside the roll, place the shredded lettuce and chopped onions. Over this place the salami, bologna, and cheese. Cover with the tomato slices, then sprinkle with the oil, pepper, and oregano. Fold the ham and place it lengthwise on the top of the hoagie. Press everything into the sandwich with a fork or knife and fold it almost closed.

Ham and Cheese Hoagie

sliced imported ham	oregano
sliced American cheese	pepper
tomato slices	chopped onions
shredded lettuce	hot peppers (optional)
oil	

On a long roll sliced lengthwise, place shredded lettuce and chopped onions. Over this, put the ham followed by the cheese. Top with the tomato slices, sprinkled with oil, oregano, and pepper.

Italian Hoagie

3 slices salami	3 slices tomato
3 slices capicola	chopped or sliced onions
3 slices Provolone cheese	oil
1 slice ham	oregano
shredded lettuce	pepper

Slice a long roll lengthwise without completely severing the top from the bottom. Inside the roll, place the shredded lettuce followed by the chopped onions. Over this, place the slices of salami, capicola, and Provolone cheese. Place the tomato slices on top of the cheese (sliced onions may be added here instead of chopped onions on the lettuce). Sprinkle with oregano, pepper, and oil. Fold the ham and lay it lengthwise on top. Using a fork or knife, press everything down into the roll more firmly and bring the top and bottom of the roll closer together (but not closed).

Variation:

1. Try adding sweet or hot peppers to the hoagie.

Three Cheese Hoagie

3 slices American cheese	chopped onions
3 slices Swiss cheese	oil
3 slices Provolone cheese	oregano
shredded lettuce	pepper
3 slices tomato	hot peppers (optional)

Slice a long roll lengthwise without completely severing the top from the bottom. Line the bottom inside of the roll with the shredded lettuce followed by the chopped onions. Over this, place the three cheeses. Top with the tomato slices sprinkled with oil, oregano, and pepper. Using a knife or fork, press everything down into the roll and bring the top and bottom closer together. Cut in half.

Tuna Salad Hoagie
tuna salad
tomato slices
chopped onions
oil
oregano
pepper
shredded lettuce

On a long roll cut lengthwise, place the shredded lettuce followed by the tuna salad. Cover with tomato slices sprinkled with oil, then add pepper, oregano, and chopped onions.

Variations:

1. Add American cheese before putting the tomatoes on the top.
2. Substitute **chicken salad** for the tuna salad.

Cheese Steak Sandwich
thin slices steak
sliced onions
3 slices Provolone cheese
cooking oil
Italian roll (or any long roll)

Sauté the onions and set them aside. Place the steaks on a hot skillet and brown on one side. They brown quickly and must be watched. When one side is done, turn the steaks over and cover them with the sautéed onions and, over them, the Provolone cheese. The roll may be toasted, if desired, by slicing down the middle, spreading the inside with butter or the drippings from the sautéed onions, and placing it for a few minutes on a hot skillet or under a broiler. When the cheese is melted, the steak should be done. Lift the steak out of the pan with the help of a spatula and slide it onto the roll, cheese side up.

Variations:

1. Steak Sandwich. Proceed as in the recipe above but use no cheese.
2. Pizza Steak. Proceed as for a cheese steak, but before placing the meat on the roll, pour hot pizza sauce or highly seasoned tomato sauce over the bread.
3. Pepper Steak. With the onions, add sweet and/or hot peppers.

4. Sautéed mushrooms may be added to the sandwich with the fried onions.

5. American cheese may be used instead of Provolone cheese.

6. Ketchup may be added as a condiment.

Eggplant "Cheese Steak"

1 eggplant (about 1½ to 2 lb. will make four sandwiches)
tomato sauce
Provolone cheese
flour
cooking oil
salt and pepper
Italian roll (or any kind of long roll)

Peel and slice the eggplant into slices ½ inch thick. Dip the pieces of eggplant into the flour seasoned with salt and pepper. Sauté in hot oil, turning each side quickly to brown. Cook until tender. Cut a long roll lengthwise and place the eggplant on the roll, then cover with the lightly seasoned hot tomato sauce, and cover this with Provolone cheese. Place under the broiler for a few minutes until the cheese melts.

Mushroom "Cheese Steak"

sliced mushrooms (generous ¼ lb. will make one sandwich)
sliced onions
tomato sauce
Provolone cheese
Italian roll (or any kind of long roll)

Sauté the mushrooms and onions in butter. Cut the roll lengthwise and toast it by spreading butter inside and placing it, open, under the broiler for a minute. Heat the tomato sauce. On the roll, place the mushrooms and onions. Pour the tomato sauce over it and cover with a few slices of Provolone cheese. Place under broiler until cheese melts.

Roast Beef "Cheese Steak"

thinly sliced roast beef, cooked
sliced onions
Provolone cheese
tomato sauce
cooking oil
Italian roll (or any kind of long roll)

On a hot skillet, sauté the onions in oil and heat the roast beef. Heat the tomato sauce separately. Slice a long roll lengthwise and place the hot roast beef and onions on it. Pour the tomato sauce over this and cover with two or three slices of Provolone cheese. Place under the broiler for a couple of minutes until the cheese melts.

Un~Sandwiches

Since most sandwiches serve as luncheon and casual dinner fare, a good part of the day would be left unaccounted for if we didn't include some ideas for breakfasts and snacks. And since not every bread-based snack or meal can rightfully be called a sandwich, the following toasts and ice cream sandwiches should be thought of an **un**-sandwiches and should make for some uncommonly good breakfasts, desserts, and wee-hour snacks.

Baltimore Toast

2 eggs, well beaten
½ cup sugar
2 cups milk
2 tsp. ground cinnamon
12 slices bread
flour
salt

Mix the eggs, sugar, milk, cinnamon, and a few grains of salt to taste. Dip the slices of bread into the mixture, then into flour. Fry in hot deep oil. Serve hot with jelly or jam.

Banana Cinnamon Toast

2 large bananas
cinnamon

Spread two slices of bread lightly with butter. Toast in a toaster oven or broiler. Peel and slice the bananas, and arrange them on the toast so that they slightly overlap each other. Sprinkle lightly with cinnamon and place under broiler for 1 or 2 minutes.

Blackberry Toast

Any kind of canned berries, including cherries, may be prepared this way.

1 can blackberries
sugar
12 slices bread
powdered sugar
nutmeg
cream
lemon, sherry or any prefered flavoring

Heat the blackberries and sweeten to taste. Place the slices of toast in bowls and pour the blackberries on top. Dust well with powdered sugar, grate a little nutmeg over, and serve hot with cream flavored with any kind of flavoring desired.

Butterscotch Toast

butter
brown sugar
cinnamon

Toast bread on one side. Cover the untoasted side with a mixture of equal parts creamed butter and brown sugar and put under the broiler until the mixture is hot and bubbly. Serve very hot, sprinkled with cinnamon.

Cheese and Bacon Toast

American cheese slices
thin bacon slices
paprika or cinnamon

Use slices of toasted white or graham bread. Place a slice of American cheese on each piece of toast. Place a thin slice of bacon on the cheese. Place in the broiler until the bacon is crisp and the cheese is melted. Serve immediately, sprinkled with paprika or cinnamon.

Cheese Toast

½ lb. American cheese
1 tsp. salt
½ tsp. prepared mustard
1 tsp. paprika
1 egg
¾ cup milk, hot

Cut the cheese into small pieces. Place in a greased pan and melt the cheese. Sprinkle with salt, paprika, and mustard. Now beat the egg slightly, add it to the milk and pour over the melted cheese. Bake in a moderate oven (350°) for 10 to 15 minutes, until the cheese is melted and a slightly brown crust has formed. Serve on any kind of toast, cut in triangles or quarters.

Cheese Toast Farmer Style
½ cup milk
½ tsp. salt
3 eggs
1 slice American or Swiss cheese
bacon fat
prepared mustard (optional)

Combine the milk, salt, and slightly beaten eggs. Put a slice of cheese between two slices of bread with the crust removed. Dip it into the egg mixture and sauté in hot bacon fat until it's golden brown on both sides. If you like it sharp, spread the cheese with mustard before covering the bread.

Cherry Toast 1
fresh cherries or a small can of pitted cherries
cream

Cut any kind of fruit or nut bread into thick fingers—about 2½ inches long and an inch thick, and toast them quickly in a hot oven so they are brown on the outside and remain soft on the inside. Heat the cherries and place in a dish. Arrange the toast fingers over them and serve with slightly sweetened cream.

Cherry Toast 2
¾ can pitted red cherries
2 Tbs. sugar
1 Tbs. flour
cinnamon
1 egg
¼ cup milk
butter or bacon fat

Heat the cherries and stir in sugar mixed with flour. Cook for a few minutes, stirring constantly. Flavor with cinnamon to taste. Dip 2 slices of bread in the mixture of beaten egg and milk and brown both sides in the butter or bacon fat. Pour the cherry sauce over the toast.

Cinnamon French Toast

1 egg
¼ cup milk
1 Tbs. ground cinnamon
flour
cooking oil

To a mixture of beaten egg and milk, add the cinnamon. Dip 2 slices of bread into this mixture, then in the flour. Fry in deep fat. Serve with jelly.

Cinnamon Toast

1 Tbs. butter
¼ cup powdered sugar
1 ½ to 2 tsp. ground cinnamon

Make a mixture of the butter, sugar, and cinnamon, creamed together well. Toast 2 slices of any kind of bread on one side and spread the untoasted side with the mixture. Broil until the mixture bubbles. Serve sizzling hot.
Variation:
1. Substitute raisin bread for plain bread.

Cinnamon Honey Toast

2 tsp. cinnamon
¼ cup honey
butter

Mix the cinnamon and honey together. Spread on hot buttered toast. Serve very hot.

English Toast

3 Tbs. cream cheese
1 Tbs. orange marmalade
butter

Toast the bread and butter it quickly. Spread with a mixture of cream cheese and marmalade. Serve at once, as hot as possible.

English Muffins

IMPORTANT—English muffins should never be cut. They should be toasted before they are opened. Before toasting, gently break the edges so that after toasting they can be readily and easily pulled apart. Butter the inside and put in the oven to be kept hot. English muffins are at their best served as hot as possible.

French Apple Sauce Toast

apple sauce, hot
butter

Cut two slices of bread into 1¼-inch thick slices. Remove the crusts; cut each slice into three strips, making an oblong block. Toast on all sides in the oven, not under a broiler or in a toaster. Dip in melted butter, and then roll quickly in thick, hot apple sauce. Serve at once.

French Griddle Toast

1 egg
¼ cup milk
sugar
butter

Dip 2 slices of bread in a mixture of egg and milk, sweetened with a few grains of sugar to taste. Cook both sides on a hot griddle with a little butter. Serve with either jelly or marmalade.

French Toast Dessert

1 egg	butter
¼ cup milk	peach halves
sugar	ground nuts (optional)
cinnamon	

Soak 2 slices of bread in an egg and milk mixture sweetened with a little sugar and cinnamon. Brown the bread in butter on both sides. Have the peaches heating up in the oven. Place half a peach on each slice of fried bread, sprinkle with cinnamon or ground nuts. Serve with a little cream on the side.

Variations:

1. Chopped dates, figs, prunes, or raisins may be added to the center of the peach.
2. Pears may be substituted for the peach halves.

French Toast Entrée

2 eggs	6 slices drained canned pineapple
⅔ cup milk	butter
salt	12 slices crisp bacon
white pepper	

Beat the eggs slightly with milk and season to taste with salt and pepper. Dip 6 slices of bread into the mixture and brown both sides on a hot griddle. Sauté the pineapple slices in butter. Serve the toast covered with pineapple slices topped with guava (or any other kind of jelly or marmalade) and garnish each with a strip of bacon.

French Toast Raisin Bread

1 egg
¼ cup milk
honey
butter
raisin bread
bread crumbs (optional)

Remove crusts from raisin bread and cut each slice in half. Dip into the egg and milk mixture sweetened to taste with honey, and brown lightly on both sides in hot butter. If you like a rough surface, after dipping the bread in the egg and milk mixture, dip into soft, fine bread crumbs. Brown and serve with syrup, honey, or jelly.

Fried Toast

Instead of toasting the bread, sauté or fry the bread in bacon fat until crisp. Try this topped with eggs and bacon.

Fruit Toast

oranges and/or pineapples, diced
sugar
lemon juice

Mix 3 Tbs. of fruit with sugar to taste, heat to the boiling point, add a few drops of lemon juice, and pour over toast.

Ginger Toast

chopped preserved ginger
few drops lemon juice
water
sugar

Have ready bread cut into 1¼-inch thick slices. Remove the crusts; cut each slice into 3 strips, making oblong blocks. Toast on all sides in the oven, and while hot, spread with a mixture made of the ginger, lemon juice, a little water, and sugar to taste. The mixture should be cooked to the consistency of marmalade. Enjoy while it is sizzling hot.

Honey Cinnamon Toast

butter
honey
coarsely chopped nuts
cinnamon

Toast 2 slices of any kind of bread. Spread with butter and honey and sprinkle generously with nuts and cinnamon. Put under the broiler for just a few seconds.

Ice Cream, Banana, and Chocolate Sandwich
waffles
vanilla ice cream
sliced banana
chopped nuts
chocolate syrup
whipped cream

Toast two waffles and cover one with the banana slices and pour over that a small amount of chocolate syrup. Cover with the ice cream and sprinkle chopped nuts and chocolate syrup over it. Top with whipped cream and cover with the last waffle.

Ice Cream and Chocolate Chips Sandwich
waffles
ice cream (any kind)
chocolate chips

Toast 2 waffles and while they're still hot sprinkle them with chocolate chips, then cover with ice cream and more chocolate chips. Top with the second waffle.

Ice Cream and Maple Nut Sandwich
waffles
vanilla ice cream
finely chopped walnuts
maple syrup

Toast two waffles and while they're still hot cover one with ice cream. Over this, sprinkle walnuts and maple syrup. Cover with the other waffle and serve immediately.

Ice Cream and Peach Sandwich
waffles
vanilla ice cream
sliced fresh peaches
whipped cream
2 tbs. liqueur (fruit flavor)
chopped nuts

Toast 2 waffles and while they're still hot cover the bottom slice with the peaches. Place the ice cream on the peaches and sprinkle it with the chopped nuts and the liqueur. Top with the whipped cream and cover with the second waffle.
Variation:
1. Use any fruit-flavored ice cream.

Ice Cream and Strawberry Sandwich

waffles
chocolate ice cream
strawberry preserves
whipped cream

Toast 2 waffles and while they're still hot spread one with strawberry preserves. Over this, place chocolate ice cream and cover with whipped cream. Top with the second waffle.

Jelly Toast Roll

jelly
day-old bread

Cut the crusts from the slices of bread and spread with jelly. Roll up as for a jelly roll. Fasten with toothpicks and place on a baking sheet. Toast under medium broiler heat, turning them until they're evenly browned.

Jocko Toast

Toast strips of French bread in the oven and then rub lightly with garlic. Very appropriate for almost any kind of chowder, fish soup, and fish stew.

Luncheon Toast

1 egg
¼ cup milk
sugar
apple sauce
powdered sugar
cinnamon
jelly

Dip each slice of bread into a mixture of egg, milk, and a little sugar to taste. Carefully transfer to a hot frying pan or a griddle greased with butter. Brown on both sides. Serve on a hot platter with apple sauce at the sides and powdered sugar and cinnamon sprinkled on top. Garnish with jelly.

Maple Sugar Toast

maple sugar
butter
whipped cream

Spread thinly sliced pieces of toast with softened butter and maple sugar. Place in the oven until the sugar melts. Serve each slice with a spoonful of whipped cream.

Marmalade Toast

Spread 2 slices of toasted bread with marmalade and heat until it's bubbling under the broiler.

Marmalade Almond Toast

marmalade
butter
toasted almonds, unsalted

Toast 2 slices of bread, spread with butter, and generously and evenly spread with marmalade. Sprinkle toasted almonds over the marmalade.

Melba Toast

Thinly slice the bread with a very sharp knife not more than ⅛ inch thick. Place on a rack in a very slow oven (200°) and allow to dry thoroughly. The toast will be done when it's crisp and a light brown color.

Milk Toast 1

1¼ to 1½ cups milk per 2 slices toast
salt and pepper
paprika

Put the toast into a bowl which has been heated; the toast may be buttered or not. Pour boiling milk over the toast and season to taste with the salt, pepper, and paprika.

Milk Toast 2

1¼ to 1½ cups milk per 2 slices toast
white sauce
salt and pepper
paprika

Put the toast into a bowl which has been heated and pour white sauce over the toast. Season to taste with salt, pepper, and paprika.
Variation:
1. Season with cinnamon instead of paprika.

Orange Toast 1

¼ cup orange juice
grated rind of 1 medium-sized orange
½ cup sugar
butter

Mix the orange juice, rind, and sugar. Spread on sizzling hot buttered toast. Put into the oven or under the broiler to brown, and serve as hot as possible.

Orange Toast 2

¼ cup orange juice
1 tsp. chopped or shredded orange rind
1 tsp. sugar
butter

Heat together the orange juice, rind, and sugar. Spread the toast with creamed butter and cut it into narrow strips. Bring the mixture to a boiling point and, just before serving, pour it over the toast. Pile crisscrossed on a hot plate.

Peanut Butter Toast

peanut butter
butter

Cream together equal parts of peanut butter and butter, and spread on very hot toast. Serve at once after cutting from corner to corner.

Pineapple Cinnamon Toast

3 Tbs. canned crushed pineapple, drained
1 tsp. brown sugar
1 tsp. cinnamon

Combine the pineapple, sugar, and cinnamon together and spread on toasted white or whole wheat bread. Place under the broiler until the mixture is slightly glazed.

Potted Meat Toast with Egg Sauce

2 Tbs. **egg sauce**
any kind of potted meat

Spread slices of toast with the potted meat and pour 2 generous Tbs. of egg sauce over the meat. Garnish with watercress.
Variations:
1. Use **cheese sauce,** tomato sauce, or **white sauce** in place of the egg sauce.

Rum Tum Ditty

½ lb. grated American cheese
1 can condensed tomato soup
½ tsp. dry mustard
1 egg

Heat the tomato soup in a double broiler and stir in the cheese until melted. Add the mustard and pour the mixture over 1 slightly beaten egg. Serve on toast.

Toasted Coconut Strips
brown sugar
butter
shredded coconut

Toast 2 slices of bread on one side and cut into strips, making 3 strips from each slice. Spread the untoasted side with a mixture of creamed butter and brown sugar, in equal parts, and brown in the oven. Sprinkle over each strip a little shredded coconut.

Tomato French Toast Cheese Sauce
1 can condensed tomato soup
2 slightly beaten eggs
salt and pepper
bacon fat
cheese sauce
paprika

Combine and mix thoroughly the tomato soup and the eggs. Season to taste with salt and pepper. Dip into the tomato mixture 8 slices of bread and cook in the bacon fat until lightly browned on both sides. Serve at once covered with cheese sauce and dusted with paprika. Garnish with watercress and a black olive.

Index